MAKE MONEY FROM KINDLE SELF-PUBLISHING

Four-Step System to Triple Your Income from Nonfiction Books

Sally Miller

FREE BONUS

As a thank you for reading my book, I've created a free workbook. With the *Zero To Bestseller* workbook you will:

> Discover how to write a nonfiction book that flies off the shelves and generates new business every single day.

> Learn the exact 12-step process to go from idea to profit in as little as 90 days using this printable PDF.

> Get the blueprint I used to write & self-publish five best sellers and reach over 16,000 readers.

Go here to receive your bonus workbook: sallyannmiller.com/ztb

Copyright © 2017-2020 Sally Miller

All rights reserved. No part of this publication may be reproduced, distributed, or transmitted in any form or by any means, including photocopying, recording, or other electronic or mechanical methods, without the prior written permission of the publisher, except in the case of brief quotations embodied in reviews and certain other non-commercial uses permitted by copyright law.

The information provided within this book is for general informational purposes only. While the author tries to keep the information up-to-date and correct, there are no representations or warranties, express or implied, about the completeness, accuracy, reliability, suitability or availability with respect to the information, products, services, or related graphics contained in this book for any purpose. Any use of this information is at your own risk.

Any advice that is provided in this book is based on the experience of the author and does not reflect the opinion of Amazon. All opinions expressed in this book are solely the opinion of the author.

Disclaimer

Some of the links in this book may be affiliate links. If you click them and decide to buy something, I may get paid a commission. This won't cost you any extra. I only include links to products or services that I either use or would happily use myself.

CONTENTS

Free Bonus 2
CHAPTER 1 8
    My Self-Publishing Story 9
    The Four-Step System 9
    Step 1: Reach Your Ideal Readers 10
    Step 2: Sell Your Book 10
    Step 3: Build Your Following 11
    Step 4: Make More Money 11
    How To Triple Your Income And More 11
    What If You Only Want To Write Books? 12
    Your Self-Publishing Story 13

Part One 14
CHAPTER 2 15
    Introducing Your WOW Statement 15
    Your Who 16
    Your Outcome 16
    Your Why 17
    Create Your WOW Statement 17
    Method 1: Online research 18
    Method 2: Ask people what they want 18
    Action Steps 19

CHAPTER 3 22
    Strategy #1: Book Promotion Sites 23
    Strategy #2: Your Email List 23
    Strategy #3: Influencers 24
    Strategy #4: Online Communities 25
    Strategy #5: Offline Networking 25
    Strategy #6: Social Media 25

Strategy #7: Paid Advertising 26
Action Steps 27

CHAPTER 4 28
How People Find Your Book 28
Categories And Best Seller Lists 29
How To Select Your Book Categories 30
Hidden Categories 31
Keywords 31
Action Steps 32

Part Two 34
CHAPTER 5 35
The Goal Of Your Book Title And Subtitle 36
The WYSIWYG Strategy 36
Curiosity Strategy 37
The Power Of A Well Crafted Subtitle 37
Testing Your Title And Subtitle 38
1. The Flow Test 38
2. The Book Cover Test 38
3. The Target Audience Test 39
Action Steps 39

CHAPTER 6 41
Elements Of Your Book Cover Design 41
Where To Find A Book Cover Designer 42
How To Write A Solid Design Brief 43
Test Your Book Cover 44
Action Steps 44

CHAPTER 7 45
Finding An Editor 45
What is Kindle Formatting? 46
Format Your Book Yourself 47
Paying Someone To Format Your Book 48
Action Steps 49

CHAPTER 8 50
Book Description Formula 50
Formatting Your Book Description 52
Action Steps 53

CHAPTER 9 54
- Two Launch Pricing Strategies 54
- Ongoing Pricing 55
- Ongoing Marketing 56
- Book Pricing Summary 58
- Action Steps 58

CHAPTER 10 59
- Verified vs. Unverified Reviews 60
- How To Get Book Reviews 60
- Amazon's Terms And Conditions 61
- Your Launch Team 61
- Action Steps 62

CHAPTER 11 63
- Your Step-By-Step Launch Plan 63
- STEP 1: Build Your Author Platform 64
- STEP 2: Create Book Cover, Edit and Format Book 65
- STEP 3: Create Launch Team 65
- STEP 4: Pre-Launch Marketing 66
- STEP 5: Set Up KDP 66
- STEP 6: Stealth Mode 67
- STEP 7: Launch Day 68
- STEP 8: Post Launch Day 68
- Two Case Studies 69
- Action Steps 70

Part Three 71

CHAPTER 12 72
- Building An Email List The Right Way 73

CHAPTER 13 76
- Features Of The Perfect Opt-In Offer 77
- Action Steps 79

CHAPTER 14 80
- Your Author Website 81
- How To Set Up Your Author Website 81
- Easy Website Tweaks To Quickly Increase Email Opt-Ins 82
- Action Steps 83

Part Four 85
CHAPTER 15 86
    1. Affiliate Sales Of Your Book 86
    2. Physical Book 87
    3. Audiobook 87
    4. More Book Titles 88
    5. Book Bundle 88
    6. Other People's Products 89
    7. Digital Training Product 89
    8. In-person Training Product 90
    9. One-On-One Service 90
    10. Speaking 91
    Action Steps 91
CHAPTER 16 92
    1. Be Consistent 92
    2. Use "Open Me" Subject Lines 93
    3. Engage Your Ideal Readers 94
    4. Use Open Loops 94
CHAPTER 17 95
    Build Know, Like, And Trust Factors 95
    Ask Subscribers To Take Action 96
    The Next Logical Step 97
CHAPTER 18 98
    Plan Your Email Sequence 99
    Your Welcome Email 99
    Write Your Follow-up Emails 101
    Test And Refine 101
    Action Steps 102
CHAPTER 19 103
Kindle terms 105
About The Author 106

CHAPTER 1

Introduction

Writing a book is hard. You agonize over every word, invest weeks researching new ideas, and spend hours in endless rounds of self-editing.

Eventually, you're ready to put your book out into the world. This is where you get stuck. Now, you face a new set of challenges.

> How do you get your book into the hands of readers?
> What if nobody likes your book?
> How much time and money will it take to publish your book?
> How can you turn all of your hard work into an <u>ongoing</u> source of income?

This last question is the most difficult to answer. There are hundreds of books and courses about self-publishing. Most teach you how to successfully launch your book. Yet, few talk about how to earn an ongoing income as an author, and there is a good reason for this. Few authors earn a living from their books.

According to a Bookscan survey, the average U.S. nonfiction book sells less than 250 copies per year. Assuming you are selling a $2.99 Kindle book, this works out at around $40 in royalties each month. An extra $40 per month is not going to pay for your kids' college education, buy your dream vacation, or help you save for retirement.

However, you can do better than the average author. In this book, I will not only show you how to earn $120 a month (triple the average earnings of a U.S. nonfiction book), I will also show you how to earn $1,000, $5,000, and even $10,000 a month.

MY SELF-PUBLISHING STORY

I'm writing this book as someone who has been in your shoes.

When I decided to publish my first nonfiction book, I didn't know where to begin. There was so much advice on the Internet, but I wished someone would tell me exactly what to do and how to make my book a best seller.

I decided to learn from people who had already published multiple best sellers, so I read books, followed experts, and signed up for the three leading self-publishing courses.

At that time, I had no existing readers and knew little about Kindle publishing. Three months later, I had written and published a best-selling book.

My first book still sells every day. Each month, I earn between $120 and $200 in royalties from one nonfiction book. Since then, I have published 16 more books. All became bestsellers in multiple Amazon categories and continue to sell today. I have reached over 50,000 readers and am building a business around my books. At the start of 2020, my monthly book royalties topped $4000. By the end of 2020 I was earning over $9000 a month from my self-published books.

But it does not stop there. I wanted to go beyond a handful of best-selling books. I have a background in email marketing, and I've helped hundreds of small business owners convert website visitors into email subscribers and loyal customers.

I applied my prior experience in online marketing to the world of self-publishing. The result is my four-step system to more than triple your income from nonfiction books.

My goal in writing this book is not to make outlandish promises. Instead, I want to show you what is possible in a relatively short time, even if you have no existing email list and little to no publishing experience.

Here is an overview of how my four-step system works.

THE FOUR-STEP SYSTEM

My system is based on the concept of a sales funnel.

A sales funnel is a visual representation of your sales process. The funnel shape indicates that more people enter the funnel than reach the end point. A sales funnel is divided into stages. The stages differ depending on your sales model.

My sales funnel for nonfiction authors has five stages:

Ideal Readers > Book Buyers > Email Subscribers > Loyal Followers > Repeat Customers

Entering the funnel are ideal readers. A percentage of these readers become book buyers, then email subscribers, then loyal followers, and ultimately repeat customers.

Your goal is to move more of your ideal readers through the funnel so they buy from you again. The more people you move through the funnel, the more lives you impact and the more money you earn. You do this by following the four steps described below.

If you're not concerned about making more money from your book, then you need only follow the first two steps in my system. These two steps will help you publish a book your readers love. However, if you want to multiply your income as a self-published author, then steps three and four are critical.

STEP 1: REACH YOUR IDEAL READERS

In step one, your goal is to help the right people discover your book. It is important you focus on your ideal readers and not just anyone. People who are not interested in your topic are unlikely to buy your book. Or worse, they may buy your book and leave a negative review.

STEP 2: SELL YOUR BOOK

Once the right people discover your book by visiting your Amazon book page, you want them to buy your book. In step two, you make your book irresistible to your ideal readers. Your aim here is to attract more readers and earn higher royalties.

STEP 3: BUILD YOUR FOLLOWING

Your following is a group of people who want to buy your books, products or services. In step three, you build a tribe who want to hear from you and who you can help.

STEP 4: MAKE MORE MONEY

Once you attract the right followers, you give them unbeatable value. You build trust over time. This leads to more sales beyond your initial book royalties.

HOW TO TRIPLE YOUR INCOME AND MORE

Let's look at some numbers to demonstrate how the system works. In the following example, the number of book buyers and new email subscribers are based on the results from my first book.

I assume that 10 percent of email subscribers purchase a $50 offering, five percent purchase a $100 offering, and one percent purchase a $500 offering. These percentages are based on my experience selling information products online. They are also the conversion rates suggested in *Internet Business Blueprint*, which is book two of the *Quit Your Job In 6 Months* series.

For now, do not worry about what the offerings are. We talk about the products and services you can create for your subscribers in chapter 15.

Here are the numbers at each stage in the sales funnel:

>   Book Buyers: 60 Kindle book sales per month at $2.99.
>   Email Subscribers: 20 new email subscribers per month.
>   Loyal Followers: 8 new email subscribers who regularly open and read your emails.
>   Repeat Customers: Two subscribers purchase a $50 offering and one purchases a $100 offering.

The ongoing monthly revenue originating from one book is as follows:

(60 book sales x $2*) + (2 sales x $50) + (1 sale x $100)
= $120 + $100 + $100 = $320

* $2 is the approximate commission you receive on a $2.99 Amazon Kindle book.

$120 in book royalties is **triple the U.S. average** of $40 each month. When you add in sales from other products and services, the total grows to $320.

The above example is conservative. My two top selling books both make over $1000 in monthly royalties. But I do not want to over promise; instead, I want to show you what's realistic when starting out. Once you become established in your space, you can introduce a high end offering such as an online course or service. Or you can focus on writing and selling more books.

Also, this example does not consider the spike in sales when you first launch your book or other offering.

Here is how a product launch may look. Fast forward two or three years and your email list now has 2,000 subscribers. You launch a new offering priced at $500. At launch alone, you make 20 sales (2,000 email subscribers multiplied by one percent).

Your income at launch is $10,000 (20 sales x $500).

WHAT IF YOU ONLY WANT TO WRITE BOOKS?

At this point, you may be thinking you just want to write books. You are an author and you have no interest in learning how to create online courses or deliver coaching services.

If this is the case, you can still use the four-step system to increase your earnings. By building a list of engaged email subscribers, you have an audience who are eager to buy your books.

In chapter 15, we will explore ten ways you can earn more money. These options include writing more books, creating book bundles, and generating other book formats.

YOUR SELF-PUBLISHING STORY

Now you understand my four-step system, it's time to create your self-publishing story. Perhaps you picked up this book because you already have a manuscript sitting on your desktop. Or maybe you have published a book on Kindle but the results have been underwhelming.

In either case, I'm here to help. In this book, I give you a step-by-step guide so that you can:

1. Quickly and easily publish your nonfiction book on Kindle.
2. Promote your book and reach thousands of readers.
3. Build a loyal following of email subscribers.
4. Maximize earnings from your first book and all your future offerings.

When you read this book you are going to save time. You can stop trying to figure things out on your own. You are also going to save money. I tell you exactly how to get your book edited and formatted without breaking the bank.

I even give you my day-by-day launch plan, which is proven to work. It is the exact plan I used to launch my first Kindle book, *Make Money On Airbnb*. My book reached over 1,500 readers in its first month and I still sell multiple copies every day.

These strategies have not just worked for me. In writing this book, I interviewed other self-published authors. I asked them exactly which promotion and monetization strategies worked for them. Their responses are included in these pages.

I urge you not to delay. Your readers are waiting to hear from you. Now is your time to become a best-selling author.

PART ONE

Step One: Reach Your Ideal Readers

CHAPTER 2

The First Step To Selling More Books

In the early 1970s, Volvo introduced the 262C. It was their first luxury coupe.

The 262C came equipped with power windows and mirrors, full leather interior, cruise control, air conditioning, heated front seats, alloy wheels, and electrically powered radio antenna.

Sales of the 262C stalled.

So Volvo increased the price and emphasized that the car was designed by Bertoni, a well-known Italian sports car designer. They re-positioned the 262C as a car that combined luxury with safety.

Volvo made no changes to the car itself. Yet, sales took off.

What does this have to do with your book?

It comes down to understanding your ideal readers so that you can position your book to sell. You may write the best book on a topic but if you fail to position it correctly, nobody will buy it.

You may think you already know who your ideal readers are. However, I encourage you not to skip this chapter. The exercise in this chapter builds the foundation for everything we discuss in the rest of the book.

INTRODUCING YOUR WOW STATEMENT

In order to explain how to position your book (or any other product) I use something I call your WOW Statement. This is a concept I have adapted from my experience teaching email marketing.

A WOW Statement is a kind of positioning statement. It allows you to control how potential readers see you and your book. This in turn wins you more readers and ultimately more money.

As you may have guessed, WOW is an acronym. It stands for:

Who: Your ideal reader.

Outcome: A positive outcome your ideal reader wants.

Why: Why you are different from other authors in your field.

Your WOW statement is used everywhere. In your book title, the description, your website copy, the emails you write, and all online and offline promotions.

Let's look at each component of the WOW Statement in more detail.

YOUR WHO

Think about who you want to read your book. It might be the type of people you feel called to serve, an earlier version of yourself, or friends and colleagues who you know will benefit from your book.

Avoid trying to write your book for *everyone*. By targeting a specific reader, you make it more appealing to that person. If you attempt to write for everyone, you create a book that appeals to no one.

With your ideal readers in mind, think about the traits they have in common. This may include some or all of the following factors:

Demographic traits (age, gender, etc.)

Values, Beliefs, Emotions

Learning Style

Occupation

Do not worry about excluding potential readers. This exercise is all about nailing who you think will most benefit from reading your book.

YOUR OUTCOME

Once you have defined your Who, you must identify exactly what your ideal reader wants. This is your Outcome.

It's time to get inside your ideal reader's head. There are two things to figure out: her most urgent problems and her secret hopes and dreams. The combination of these two things leads you to the desired outcome you can provide for your reader.

Do not jump on the first problem you encounter. You want to dig deep until you find the core issue. What do I mean by this? Ultimately, people desire more money, more health, more time, or more love.

For example, small business owners want more customers and not better copywriting skills. The latter is simply one way to solve the core problem.

If you help people improve their copywriting skills, focus your marketing message around the desirable end result. This may be a larger audience, more followers, or more sales. *A Step-By-Step Guide To Writing Copy That Sells* is more persuasive than *How To Improve Your Copywriting Skills*.

YOUR WHY

Lastly, we look at your Why. This is the most important part of your WOW Statement. Yet, it is often overlooked.

Your Why is how you differentiate yourself from the competition.

Frist and foremost, your Why is about you. So think about how you are unique. Also think about what other authors do and how you can be different. The combination of your uniqueness and what other authors do is your Why.

Here is an example from the business world. Jetblue is all about customer service. The company even has a Customer Bill of Rights. Part of their Customer Bill of Rights states that:

> *"JetBlue Airways exists to provide superior service in every aspect of our customer's air travel experience."*

Other airlines focus on price or flying their customers anywhere. JetBlue differentiate themselves by providing a high level of comfort and service at an affordable price.

CREATE YOUR WOW STATEMENT

You may still be wondering how exactly you create your WOW Statement. There is one thing you must not do: Do not make it up!

Marketers often ask you to *imagine* your ideal customer. I prefer a research-based approach. There are two methods you can use to find out more about your ideal readers.

METHOD 1: ONLINE RESEARCH

This involves visiting sites relevant to your field. Examples include forums, online groups, Q&A sites, and review sites.

The best way to start is by looking at the Amazon reviews of books similar to yours. Pay particular attention to two- and three-star reviews. Note any specific examples of what people like and dislike.

If you have an existing audience, you can also review the questions your followers ask most often. For example, if you write a blog, read your blog comments and look for common themes. If you have an email following, review past inquiries your subscribers have sent you. We talk more about building a following in chapters 12 through 14.

METHOD 2: ASK PEOPLE WHAT THEY WANT

The second research method is to ask your ideal readers directly. You can meet potential customers for coffee, chat with them online, or send them a written survey.

One quick and simple exercise is to post a question on your Facebook page or personal profile. Then follow up with a few individuals via messenger.

When talking with people, make sure you ask open-ended questions. Your goal is to explore your target audience's urgent problems and secret hopes and dreams.

Below are some example questions you could ask your ideal readers. Problem X is the specific problem your nonfiction book solves.

> Can you tell me about the last time you experienced problem X?
> How did it make you feel?
> What, if anything, have you done to solve that problem?
> What do you like or dislike about the solutions you have tried?

The above questions are for your ideal readers. It is important you understand their specific challenges and do not assume you already know the answers. This exercise helps you connect deeply with the people you want to help.

Capture as much detail as possible. Make sure you write everything down, either in a Word document or on paper. Also write down the specific language your ideal readers use. This level of detail is invaluable when writing your book description, emails, website copy, and more.

In the action steps below, I show you how to take your research and come up with your complete WOW Statement.

ACTION STEPS

Throughout this book, I ask you to take action. I encourage you to complete these exercises because they will help you successfully launch your nonfiction book and earn more money.

1. Spend time getting to know your ideal readers. Use one or more of the research methods described above to find out about their urgent problems and secret dreams.

2. Now you have a clear picture, describe your ideal reader as fully as possible. Your description may include demographics, emotions, values, beliefs, occupations, learning style, opinions, and more.

Note that your ideal reader does not have to be defined by demographics. For example, your ideal reader may be a single professional who feels stuck in the corporate world and yearns to create a lifestyle business that can be managed from any location.

Write down your description. This is your Who.

3. Next, refer back to your research and answer the following three questions.

> What are your ideal reader's urgent problems? Example: "I hate looking in the mirror, and I hate the way my body looks."
> What are your ideal reader's secret hopes and dreams? Example: "I wish I looked the way I did when I first met my husband. I just want to look good in a swimsuit again."
> What is your ideal reader's dream solution that she would pay almost anything for? Example: "If only there

> was a way I could lose 10 pounds without giving up my favorite food or going to the gym for an hour every day."

Take your answers from these three questions and describe the biggest result you can provide your ideal reader. This is your Outcome.

4. Now it's time to look within and define your Why. To define your Why, you want to discover what makes you uniquely you. Answer the following questions:

> What three things make you memorable? For example, it might be an unusual quirk, a unique experience, your background, a prior occupation, your hobbies, or something else.
> What are your special talents? These are often things you have been good at since childhood.
> What do people always compliment you on, or seek your advice about?
> What do other authors in your field do that you can do differently?

Take the answers to these questions and describe why you are unique within your field. This is your Why.

5. After completing steps one through four, review your WOW Statement as a whole. Make sure you are able to answer yes to all of the following questions regarding your statement:

> Does it clearly define a target market?
> Does it use the language of my target market?
> Does it differentiate me from other people in the same space?
> Is it credible and can I deliver on its promise?
> Does it leave room for growth?

Your WOW Statement will evolve over time, so don't worry about making it perfect.

Here is a simple WOW Statement from the business world:

> *"For upscale American families, Volvo is the family automobile that offers maximum safety."*

In the upcoming chapters, we look at how to use your WOW Statement to attract more of your ideal readers and sell more books.

CHAPTER 3

Find Your Readers Online And Offline

Amazon has approximately 300 million active accounts. That is an impressive pool of potential customers. Yet, Amazon shoppers are unlikely to discover your recently published book on their own.

You need to set the ball rolling.

When you launch a new title, your initial goal is to direct as many potential readers as possible to your Amazon book page. This chapter discusses seven ways you can do this. Later in the book, we discuss how to incorporate these strategies into your launch plan.

Luckily, you do not have to *heavily* promote your book forever. Once you demonstrate that people buy your title, Amazon will lend a helping hand and start promoting your book for you.

NOTE: In 2020, it is no longer the case that you can launch a book and then rely on Amazon to do all the heavy lifting. This is especially true in the more competitive genres. You may get lucky. You may stumble upon an under-served niche where organic sales are still possible. My Airbnb book still sells today without any promotion on my part. But in most niches, you will need to keep marketing your book so that sales don't dry up.

We discuss ongoing marketing tactics and how the Amazon engine works in future chapters.

So how do you help your ideal readers find your book on Amazon?

STRATEGY #1: BOOK PROMOTION SITES

A promotion site builds a list of people who enjoy book deals. For a fee, typically between $5 and $100, they share your book with their followers.

If you do not have a large audience, leveraging promotion sites is the fastest way to reach new readers. One author told me how important promotion sites were to her.

The day Mimi Emmanuel launched her book, *My Story Of Survival*, her Internet connection went down. She couldn't email her launch team, post on social media, or contact influencers. It could have been a disaster. Yet, her book was downloaded over 2,000 times in the first couple of days. This is largely due to the paid promotions that Mimi had the foresight to schedule in advance.

When applying to book promotion sites, remember that not all promotions are equal. Your book genre impacts how successful a promotion is. I recommend browsing promotion sites and seeing which ones appeal to your target readers.

The time of year can also influence the effectiveness of a promotion. For example, if your ideal readers start healthy habits around the New Year, that's a good time to promote your fitness book.

In my free [Zero To Bestseller workbook](), I share a list of promotion sites that have worked for me and for other self-published authors. I periodically update this list as I get feedback from the indie author community.

STRATEGY #2: YOUR EMAIL LIST

If you already have a following, these are the people most likely to buy your book. Your email subscribers enjoy your content and have already asked to hear from you.

I recommend emailing your list two or three times prior to launch day. Share your progress and get people excited about your new book. On the day your book is published, your subscribers will be amongst the first to download it.

I also suggest you create a special list of people who agree to support you. This is your launch team. We discuss launch teams in depth in chapters ten and eleven. For now, understand that your launch team is separate from your main email list.

STRATEGY #3: INFLUENCERS

The third way to promote your book is to reach out to influencers in your field. For example, you may get featured on podcasts or write guest posts.

Make sure you target people who have a large and relevant audience. In chapter two you did some research to identify your ideal readers. Hopefully, you visited websites and online communities where your ideal readers gather. The owners of these resources are the people you want to reach out to.

You may feel intimidated contacting influencers, especially if they are well known. Below is one strategy I've used that makes the process easier.

Start by contacting experts you have referenced in your book. In your initial email, do not ask for anything. Simply tell the person about your book and ask for permission to reference their work. Here is an email template I used to write to influencers in my field.

> *Hi [name],*
> *I wanted to reach out to say thank you for everything you've shared about [topic]. You have been a great inspiration to me. [Insert example of how their website, podcast, or community outreach has helped you].*
> *I'm now sharing what I've learned with others and would love to include your story in my new book. Would this be okay?*
> *My book is [book title and subtitle].*
> *I'd also include a link to your website so that my readers can find out more about you. And of course, I'd send you an advance reader copy of my book.*
> *Would you please let me know if this would be all right? My planned publication date is [launch date].*
> *Thank you again for being an inspiration!*
> *Kind Regards,*
> *Sally Miller*

Everybody I contacted using the above template gave me permission to mention them in my book. Several also asked if they could help me in any way. This is when I sent a follow-up email with a request.

The request can be small, such as asking them to share your book on social media. Or it may be big, like requesting a podcast interview. Make sure you only ask for one action. This makes it easier for the influencer to say yes.

STRATEGY #4: ONLINE COMMUNITIES

The fourth strategy is to make connections in relevant online communities, such as Facebook groups. It's important to spend time being helpful before sharing your book in a group. Avoid being overly self-promotional. I recommend being active in a group for at least two weeks prior to asking for support. Once you build up goodwill, people are eager to help you by buying (and reviewing) your book.

A more advanced strategy is to create your own online community. Barry Watson, author of *Relationship Rehab*, *Strong Women in Bad Relationships*, and *Rock Solid Relationship*, created a Facebook Group for author entrepreneurs. Through his group, Barry is building meaningful and valuable connections within the author community.

Creating an effective online group takes time. You need to give value and foster a sense of community. Barry does this by organizing online events, sharing tips, and encouraging mutual support between group members.

STRATEGY #5: OFFLINE NETWORKING

Connecting with people offline is powerful. When people meet you in person they are excited to read your book. Deidre Edwards, author of *Toolkit For Wellness*, handed out bookmarks to promote her new book. She carried the bookmarks with her at all times. This strategy works well because it's personal and gives people a tangible reminder to read your book. Deidre still benefits from an ongoing stream of sales generated by her bookmarks.

STRATEGY #6: SOCIAL MEDIA

If you have a business following, sharing your book on social media is an easy way to drive traffic to your Amazon page. You can get people excited about your upcoming launch by sharing regular updates. For example, ask your followers to vote on different book covers. Also share progress, such as the number of downloads and reviews, throughout your launch week.

If your book becomes an Amazon best seller or is featured as a hot new release, capture a screenshot. These make great visuals to share with friends and followers. Best sellers and hot new releases will be explained further in chapter four.

If you don't have a business following, you can still share on your personal accounts. However, this is less effective. While your friends and family may want to support you, not all of them are your ideal readers.

STRATEGY #7: PAID ADVERTISING

Before we discuss paid advertising, a word of caution: If you're just starting out, I do not recommend you pay for advertising. It's all too easy to sink money and see little or no return.

I have had success with paid advertising, including Amazon Ads and Facebook Ads. But not every campaign of mine has yielded results. I prefer to use Facebook advertising to build my following and not to sell a book. Whereas, Amazon Advertising can be an effective way to maintain your book sales once you've proven readers want to buy your title.

Here is how I used Facebook Ads to build my following before selling a book:

Facebook Ad -> Landing Page On Your Website -> Email Sign-Up -> Sequence of Emails Leading Up To Book Launch

The landing page has an email sign-up form with an opt-in offer. For example, you can offer a free or discounted copy of your new book in return for an email address. Then, follow up with a series of engaging emails before asking someone to buy your book.

We discuss opt-in offers in chapter 13. Chapter 14 talks about how to create a landing page and chapter 18 teaches you how to write an email sequence that sells.

ACTION STEPS

1. Read through the above strategies and select three or four you can use to launch your book. Make sure you consider your resources. For example, how much time do you have to promote your book? Do you have an existing audience? Do you have relationships with influencers in your field? At a minimum, I recommend you utilize book promotion sites and a launch team.

In chapter 11, you will learn how to incorporate these strategies into a launch plan.

Promoting your book can be hard work, but it's worth it. If you launch your book successfully, Amazon markets your book for you. You can start earning income from your first Kindle book. The next chapter will explain exactly how this works.

CHAPTER 4

Let Amazon Find Your Readers For You

Imagine this: You wake up, log on to the Kindle Direct Publishing Platform (KDP), and check your reports. While you were asleep, you sold three, five, or even ten copies of your book.

I sell copies of my books every day. Some days, I sell 20 books and on other days I sell hundreds. While this income is not entirely passive, it does come with minimal ongoing promotion on my part. NOTE: I no longer believe in completely passive income. The more you do to promote your books (or other offerings) the faster your income will grow. The key is to implement marketing activities that generate the greatest return on investment.

Once you understand how the Amazon engine works, you can set your book up to sell with just a little supervision from you. In this chapter, I show you how to use categories and keywords to help people find your book on Amazon.

HOW PEOPLE FIND YOUR BOOK

There are four main ways a casual browser can find your book in the Kindle store (without you having to pay for advertising). The first three relate to your book's ranking. The fourth is impacted by its keywords. I explain both concepts later in this chapter.

The four main ways an Amazon user can find your book are:

1. **Best Seller Lists:** This is where someone visits the Kindle store and scrolls down through the various categories. To appear high in a category, you need to climb the best seller list for that category.

2. **Suggested Books:** These are displayed in the "Customers who bought this item also bought" section when browsing a product on Amazon. Suggested books also appear in targeted emails sent to Amazon users.

3. **New Releases:** These are displayed in the top right hand corner for each category. New Releases are newly launched books that sold the most copies in the current month. You can only appear in the New Release list during the first month after your book is published.

4. **Keyword Search:** This is where a casual browser types a word or phrase into the Amazon search bar and then browses the results.

CATEGORIES AND BEST SELLER LISTS

Book categories are best understood via an example. If you visit the Kindle Store on Amazon, you will see that Kindle books are organized in a hierarchy. For example, at the top level there is a category called "Nonfiction." Within "Nonfiction," you see "Arts & Photography," "Biographies & Memoirs," "Business & Investing," and so on.

You can drill down into increasingly specific sub-categories. Here's an example of a category tree:

> Kindle Store > Kindle eBooks > Business & Money > Entrepreneurship & Small Business > Marketing

Each category has a best seller list. So your book may be ranked 10,000 in all paid books, yet be the number four best seller in the Marketing category. Your book's ranking is based on sales of your book relative to the sales of other books.

Furthermore, there are two Kindle stores: the free store and the paid store. Each store has its own best seller list. Your book appears in just one store, depending on whether it's free or paid. Your ranking in the free store has no impact on your ranking in the paid store, and vice versa. So if your book has a good sales history, you don't want to lose this by switching from paid to free.

To find the ranking for a book, scroll down the Amazon book page until you see the section titled "Product Details." At the end of this section you find "Amazon Best Sellers Rank." Here is an example:

Amazon Best Sellers Rank: #65,689 Paid in Kindle Store
#27 in Kindle Store > Kindle eBooks > Business & Money > Entrepreneurship & Small Business > Marketing
#51 in Kindle Store > Kindle eBooks > Business & Money > Entrepreneurship & Small Business > Small Business

If your book reaches the number one position in any category, it receives a best seller tag. This is the orange ribbon you see on some books. Many, including myself, believe the best seller tag helps you sell more books. The ribbon makes your book stand out in the Kindle store and shows potential buyers that your book is popular.

In summary, books with a high sales ranking are more likely to be seen by potential readers. If you reach the top ten in your category, your book appears on the first page. Even better, if your book reaches number one, it receives the orange best seller tag.

HOW TO SELECT YOUR BOOK CATEGORIES

When you set up your book in KDP, you select two categories. You want to pick categories that help your ideal readers find your book in the Kindle store. For example, a small business owner researching online marketing may browse the following category tree: Business & Money > Entrepreneurship & Small Business > Marketing. If your book discusses social media for local businesses, then "Marketing" would be a good category choice.

There are three criteria to consider when selecting your categories. Make sure each choice is:

1. Relevant to your book topic. This is the most important criteria. Spend time browsing the different categories and see where your book best fits.

2. The lowest sub-category in a relevant category tree. Your book appears in the sub-category you select and every category above it. By picking a low level option, your book is featured in more places in the Kindle store. This gives shoppers more opportunities to discover your book.

3. The lowest competition category that is also relevant. When you pick a low competition category, your book has a high chance of ranking in the top ten. Top ten books appear on the first page. To establish competitiveness, look at the book ranking for the top three books in your target category. If the number three book has a ranking greater than 50,000, your book can easily break into the top three.

In summary, select book categories that are relevant, low level, and low competition. Competitiveness should be your last consideration. Never sacrifice relevancy for an easy to rank category.

HIDDEN CATEGORIES

When you set up your book, you may notice a mismatch between the categories in the Kindle Store and the options available to you in KDP. These "hidden categories" create a problem. What should you do if the category you want is not visible in the KDP set-up screen?

You have a few courses of action. First, you can guess at which category matches the one you are targeting. Most of the time your best guess is correct.

You can also look at this help article on Amazon's website. It has a section which explains how to get your book listed in categories with keyword requirements.

Lastly, if neither of the above strategies work, you can contact KDP support. Tell them which category you would like to list your book in and why. You can send KDP support an online message by clicking the "Contact Us" button on the lower left of the KDP help screen.

KEYWORDS

Categories are not the only way your book is found in the Kindle store. Many Amazon users start by typing something in the search box. For example, a person may search for the term "passive income" in the Kindle book store. "Passive income" is an example of a keyword or phrase.

When you set up your book in KDP, you can select seven keywords. These should be terms you think your ideal readers search for when looking for a book on your topic.

Here is the step-by-step system I use to find keywords for my books:

1. First identify keywords using a keyword search tool such as KW Finder. Start by typing in a possible keyword, for example "Passive Income." The tool tells you the number of monthly Google searches for that term. It also suggests other related terms. These are all candidate keywords for your book.

2. Once you have ten or more keyword ideas, visit Amazon.com. Start typing a keyword into Amazon's search bar. Amazon gives you suggestions ordered by

popularity. For example, if you type "Passive," you see "Passive Income," "Passive Income Ideas" and "Passive Income Online." If you want to go deeper, you can also use a tool called Publisher Rocket. This online tool displays Amazon monthly search volume for the keywords you enter. However it is a paid tool.

3. Pick seven relevant keywords that are popular on Amazon, which your book has a chance to rank for.

4. Put those seven keywords into the KDP set-up screen.

5. After a week or more, visit Amazon's website and try searching for each keyword you selected. If your book is on the first page, congratulations! Your book can be found by users searching for that topic. If your book is not on the first page, investigate why this might be.

Amazon's engine looks for keywords in the KDP keyword field but also in other places such as the book title, description, and reviews. Take a look at the top ranking books for your keyword. If the highest ranking books all have the keyword in the title, they are difficult to compete with.

If necessary, try changing some of your keywords. I like to switch one keyword at a time so that I can see what works and what doesn't. Here is an example to show you how the process works.

I started with "Passive Income" as one of the keywords for my Airbnb book. My book was not ranking for that search term. It is hugely competitive and the first few pages are filled with books that have passive income in the title.

I switched the keyword to "Passive Income Ideas." This is more specific, and therefore less competitive. At one point I reached page three for that keyword. Since then, my book has slipped to page five and sometimes lower.

Relevancy is another factor that determines how high your book ranks for a particular keyword. If few people click on your book after searching for a specific keyword, then Amazon determines that keyword is not relevant to your book. This is probably why my book is not ranking high for the term "Passive Income Ideas."

In contrast, my book appears on the front page for the term "Airbnb." This is because the word "Airbnb" is in the title and is highly relevant to my book.

ACTION STEPS

1. Follow the steps in this chapter to select your two book categories.
2. Follow the steps in this chapter to select your seven keywords.

This brings us to the end of step one: Reach Your Ideal Readers. You have created your WOW Statement and understand how to help the right people find your book. In the next section, you learn how to sell more books by making your book irresistible to your ideal readers.

PART TWO

Step Two: Sell Your Book

CHAPTER 5

Give Your Book An Irresistible Title

"I don't think the job of packaging is to please your boss. I think you must please the retailer, but most of all, attract and delight and sell to the browsing, uncommitted new customer." – Seth Godin

These are the words of Seth Godin, published on his popular blog in 2010.

Packaging sells. This is especially true in the Kindle store where your book must compete with millions of others to grab the attention of shoppers.

In this section, you learn how to make your book irresistible to your ideal readers, starting with the title and subtitle. But first, an important side note. You can package something to look pretty, but if your product doesn't deliver, then you fail your readers and yourself. Please do not create a low quality book and dress it up as something else.

If you're unsure whether your book is good enough, refer to the WOW Statement you created in chapter two. Ask yourself these two questions:

1. Is the outcome in your WOW Statement something your ideal readers want?
2. Does your book deliver on this promise?

If you answer yes to both these questions, you are good to go. If you cannot answer in the affirmative, spend some time refining your book to give your ideal readers the best possible result.

THE GOAL OF YOUR BOOK TITLE AND SUBTITLE

Your book title wants to do two things.

First, it must appeal to your ideal readers and get them to click on your title. You want to tell them what they get from reading your book. This is the same as the outcome from your WOW Statement.

Second, it should help readers find your book on Amazon. You do this by using keywords. We discussed keyword selection in chapter four. Where appropriate, you want to incorporate one or more of these keywords into your title and subtitle.

So how do you achieve these goals?

When you set up your book in KDP, you have two fields to play with: Book Name and Subtitle. I call these two fields "title" and "subtitle." For example, the title of this book is: *Make Money from Kindle Self-Publishing*. The subtitle is: *Four-Step System to Triple Your Income from Nonfiction Books*.

Below are two strategies you can use to create an irresistible title. Later, we discuss how to craft the ideal subtitle.

THE WYSIWYG STRATEGY

I have borrowed the term WYSIWYG from the software industry. It stands for What You See Is What You Get. A WYSIWYG application enables you to see on screen exactly what will appear when a document is printed.

In my WYSIWYG strategy, you name your book after the exact outcome it delivers. I like this approach because it is simple and direct. For example, this book is called *Make Money from Kindle Self-Publishing*. You can't get clearer than that.

The title of this book also incorporates the keyword "Kindle Self-Publishing." Remember, a keyword is a phrase that someone types into a search bar. Imagine an Amazon user wants to find a book about selling crafts on Etsy. That person might search for "how to sell on Etsy." The phrase "how to sell on Etsy" is a keyword.

If you can, incorporate keywords into your title or subtitle. This helps people find your book when searching for your topic on Amazon. However, *do not* incorporate keywords at the cost of clarity.

CURIOSITY STRATEGY

The second strategy for coming up with your book title is to use intrigue. This works because it entices people to click on your book to find out more. It takes advantage of a psychological phenomenon called the "curiosity gap." This is the gap between something a person knows and something she wants to know. Making a person aware of the gap creates a desire to acquire the missing information.

Here are some examples of books that use curiosity in the title:

> *10% Happier* – Can a book teach me how to increase my happiness by 10 percent?
> *The Upside of Irrationality* – Is there an unexpected benefit to being irrational?
> *When to Rob a Bank* – What is this book really about?

As you can see, the above titles catch your attention as a reader. They entice you to explore further by clicking on the title to find out more.

THE POWER OF A WELL CRAFTED SUBTITLE

Regardless of which approach you take with your title, the subtitle is your opportunity to sell. If your book is nonfiction, this is where you make your big promise. Ask yourself these questions:

1. How will someone's life be changed by reading your book?
2. What significant outcome does your book offer?

It bears repeating: Please do not make a promise you cannot meet. While you want to go big, if your book fails to deliver, this will result in negative reviews.

Here are some books with subtitles that make a big promise:

> *The 4-Hour Workweek: Escape 9 – 5, Live Anywhere, And Join The New Rich*

The $100 Startup: Reinvent the Way You Make a Living, Do What You Love, and Create a New Future

Rock Solid Relationship: 7 Ways to Build Lasting Love That Will Take Your Marriage or Dating Life From Ho-Hum to Amazing

TESTING YOUR TITLE AND SUBTITLE

If you are having a hard time coming up with titles, try giving your brain a rest. By taking a break, your sub-conscious continues to work on the problem and present new ideas to you.

I recommend spending a week or more brainstorming. Your first book title is rarely your best idea, so aim to come up with ten or more potential titles.

When you have multiple title and subtitle combinations, you need to test them. The following are three tests you can use to select your final title and subtitle.

1. THE FLOW TEST

Start by saying your title and subtitle out loud. Ask yourself:

> Is it awkward to say, or does it flow easily?
> Are any of the words difficult to pronounce?

Your book title should be memorable. This makes it easy for people to share your book with their friends. An awkward sounding title is forgettable. It can also put a potential reader off.

2. THE BOOK COVER TEST

Next, your title should fit your book cover. It should be easy to read when the cover image is scaled down to thumbnail size.

Take a look at Amazon and browse through the Kindle store. Notice how a clearly visible title invites you to click on the book to find out more.

3. THE TARGET AUDIENCE TEST

Your title must appeal to your target reader. This is the most important test. Make sure you avoid unfamiliar jargon and words your audience may find embarrassing or off-putting. A memorable book title (one that readers recommend to their friends) is simple and easy to say.

Also, do not rely on your own opinion. You need to ask your target audience. There are various ways you can do this. The following are two methods I use.

The first approach is to ask directly. Make sure you ask your target audience, rather than those who would never buy your book. Join Facebook Groups or forums where your ideal readers congregate. Make a post and ask people which title and subtitle combination they prefer. This is a quick way to gather a lot of feedback.

One downside of this approach is something I call the social effect. People do not want to disappoint and may say they like a title when in reality they find it unappealing. Also, people are easily influenced, sometimes without realizing it. For example, a title may emerge as a favorite because a few influential people gave it positive feedback. This leads to more people selecting the same title as their favorite.

The second testing method overcomes these issues. In this approach, you create an anonymous poll. You can use a free tool like SurveyMonkey or Typeform.

When you build your survey, start by giving a brief description of your book. This context helps people give you more meaningful feedback. Next, create a multiple choice question asking people to select the one title and subtitle combination they like best. Lastly, include an optional field where people can give additional feedback. For example, you can ask whether they would make any changes to the title they picked.

Share your survey in targeted communities where you ideal readers gather. You may get fewer responses than if you ask people directly. However, the responses are more likely to be an honest reflection of people's preferences.

ACTION STEPS

1. Brainstorm ten or more title and subtitle combinations for your book.

2. Test your title and subtitle and pick a favorite.

Once you have your winning title and subtitle, you are ready to create your book cover. In the next chapter, you will learn how to create a book cover your ideal readers will love.

CHAPTER 6

Create A Book Cover That Sells

For Kindle books, a well-designed cover is critical. If you doubt my word, take a look at Amazon. Browse the Kindle store and notice how some books jump off the screen. They invite you to check them out now. These are the books that get more clicks, more downloads, and more reviews.

In order to maximize the potential of a platform like Amazon, you must capture the attention of the casual browser. This is the primary role of your book cover.

ELEMENTS OF YOUR BOOK COVER DESIGN

Your book cover has several components. The first is your title and subtitle. In the previous chapter, you chose the perfect title for your book. Now you need to put that title on your front cover. Make sure the text is big and bold. It's essential that the title and subtitle are readable at thumbnail size as displayed in the Kindle store.

The second component of your design is color. One option is to select contrasting colors like black and yellow. These bold colors stand out on Amazon's white background. Alternatively, you can do as I do and opt for a simple, white cover. White or light covers look uncluttered and appeal to certain target readers.

A helpful website is colorlovers.com. Use this site to search for color palettes you find appealing.

The third element of your book cover is the image. Note you do not have to use an image. Many successful books have text only covers. One famous example is *The 7 Habits of Highly Effective People*.

If you decide to use an image, I recommend making it less visible than the title. Your title is the easiest way to communicate your message. Your image should support your title but not overshadow it.

Lastly, ensure you have permission to use the image. You can do this by purchasing an image from a stock photo site like iStock. Read the licensing rules before you purchase. Make sure the image can be used for commercial purposes. You also have the option of using an image you already own, such as a photograph or hand-drawn picture.

WHERE TO FIND A BOOK COVER DESIGNER

If you are a graphic designer, go ahead and create your own book cover. You can find the relevant image dimensions and other details on Amazon's help pages.

However, most of us are not designers. So what do we do?

First, please do not attempt to create a book cover yourself. There are many places you can get an affordable cover that looks professional. If you have spent any time browsing the Kindle Store, then you know how an amateurish cover can stop you from buying.

The most affordable place to hire a cover designer is Fiverr. This is a website where you can purchase services starting at five dollars. The site is easy to use and it is free to create an account. Start by searching for the term "book covers" and then browse the available gigs (this is Fiverr's name for services).

Fiverr sellers vary in experience and quality. Look at reviews to make sure the Fiverr gig is established and has a track record of delivering a quality product. Also ask in author groups or forums for personal recommendations.

It is a good idea to get two or three designs. Later in this chapter we discuss how to test your candidate book covers.

A second option is 99designs. This is more expensive, but you can get over 30 professional book cover designs for as little as $300.

99designs allows you to create a design brief and ask professionals to submit sample book covers. You can vote for the ones you like best and request changes to the initial submissions. You can also ask other people to vote on your designs.

Lastly, you can hire a designer direct. This is what I do. Try asking for recommendations in author groups, or contract through an established company like Archangel Ink.

HOW TO WRITE A SOLID DESIGN BRIEF

Regardless of what method you use to find a cover designer, you need to clearly communicate what you want. You can do this by writing a design brief.

Here are the elements of a good design brief:

1. Book title and subtitle.
2. Two or three sentences summarizing your book.
3. A brief description of your ideal reader and how you want them to feel when reading your book.
4. Preferred colors (if any).
5. Preferred image(s) if you have one.
6. Example books that have covers similar to what you want.

Item six is the fastest way to communicate the look and feel you are aiming for. It isn't strictly necessary. A good designer can interpret your written requirements and often surprise you by creating something remarkable that is unlike anything you envisioned. But if you have a strong concept, I recommend providing examples of covers you like.

Here is a simple design brief I used for my first book.

> *My book is called "Make Money On Airbnb: How To Quickly & Easily Earn $2,500 A Month From Your Home." It's a how-to book aimed at people looking to earn a side income. My book gives them the knowledge and motivation to list their home on Airbnb and make good money hosting.*
>
> *I like simple and clean looking book covers where the title pops. Some book covers I like are: "You Are a Writer" and "The Art of Work" both by Jeff Goins, "Thinking Fast and Slow" by Daniel Kahneman, and "Drive" by Daniel Pink.*

As you can see from the above example, your design brief does not need to be complex. This is especially true if you provide a selection of covers you like.

TEST YOUR BOOK COVER

Once you have some designs you like, it's time to test them. A good designer will send you more than one sample cover. If you use Fiverr, I recommend buying several Fiverr gigs to give yourself options.

The first test is the size test. View each cover image on screen. Reduce the dimensions to thumbnail size. Then make sure the title and subtitle are clearly readable. Also look to see if the cover "pops." I like to position the thumbnail image next to the relevant category in Amazon's Kindle store. I check to see if my cover stands out among similar books.

Second, you want to test whether your cover appeals to your target audience. You can either share your book covers in online forums or use an anonymous survey.

This is the same process we discussed in the previous chapter for testing your book title and subtitle. Follow the steps outlined in chapter five but instead of positing sample book titles, share your book cover images. Then ask people to vote on their favorite.

Sharing your book covers is an excellent way to get feedback on what your target audience responds to. It also helps build excitement for your upcoming book launch. People love to be involved in a launch and are more likely to support you when the big day finally arrives.

ACTION STEPS

1. Decide how you want to get your cover created. Some options include Fiverr, 99designs, an individual graphic designer, or a book cover design service.

2. Write and submit your book cover design brief.

We are now done with your book cover. The next chapter will focus on how to get your book edited and formatted. I will explain why it's important to use a professional book editor, and I will also share how to hire a professional team without breaking the bank.

CHAPTER 7

All About Editing And Formatting

Sending your book to an editor can be daunting. You may not want to send your book to *anyone*. You might tell yourself that one more day of self-edits will ensure perfection. You may be scared to show your book to a professional. What if it's not good enough?

These concerns are normal. However, your editor is your friend. She provides a professional and objective view of your book, spots errors you could never find on your own, and guarantees you will publish a professional, high-quality product.

You have already spent the time writing a quality manuscript. You have also created a book cover that sells. Professional editing and formatting are the next steps to differentiate your book from the scores of similar titles on Amazon.

FINDING AN EDITOR

A professional editor may charge anywhere from $50 to $5,000 for a 20,000 word book. It does not always follow that the more you pay, the better the service. Below is a process you can follow to find the right editor for you at a price you can afford.

First, you want to make sure your editor performs both a content edit and a copyedit of your book. A content edit identifies gaps in your book and reviews the overall flow. A copyedit focuses on each word, sentence, and paragraph. An editor who performs both services:

> improves the structure and organization of your sentences;
> improves clarity and readability;

> ensures you use a consistent voice;
> highlights any redundancies, inconsistencies, incorrect grammar usage, and confusing passages;
> checks your book for overall flow, including flow from one chapter to the next;
> makes suggestions using the Track Changes functionality in your preferred word processor (so that you can easily review suggestions and accept or reject them).

The first place you want to look for an editor is in author communities. Personal recommendation is the best way to find any professional, whether it is a cover designer, editor, or formatter. If you do not have any author connections, you can hire a freelancer using Fiverr or Upwork. We discussed Fiverr in the previous chapter. Upwork is one of many services that connect freelancers with jobs.

Regardless of where you look for an editor, make sure they have prior experience editing books like yours. You can ask to see samples of their work. Also, be sure to request an exact quote up front. A quote is typically based on the number of words in your manuscript, but not every editor uses the same approach to pricing.

Finally, find someone you like, who fits your style of working. The best way to do this is to request a sample edit. I recommend you shortlist at least three editors. Then ask each one to do a sample edit of the same pages. Some editors do this for free. Others may charge a nominal fee (less than $30). Compare the sample edits and ask the following questions:
> Which editor best understands your book and your message?
> Who made the most recommendations that improve the quality of your book?
> Who would you most enjoy working with?

Lastly, make sure you agree to a timeframe as well as a fee before making your final choice. I attempt to complete two or three rounds of edits in a two-week period. This is quite aggressive and you may prefer to take a little longer. Whatever timeframe you agree on, you need to be confident that your editor can complete edits in time for your planned launch date.

WHAT IS KINDLE FORMATTING?

Once you have a professionally edited manuscript, it's time to format your book.

Formatting does two things. First, it ensures that your book has a readable font, properly formatted number and bullet lists, clean looking chapter headings, and more. Second, it converts your manuscript into a format that can be uploaded into KDP.

If you have ever bought a Kindle book and found yourself irritated by inconsistent margins or random blank pages, then you understand how important this step is. A poorly formatted book attracts negative reviews which ultimately kills your sales.

You can either format your book yourself or pay someone to do it for you. In the following sections, I describe these options in more detail so you can decide which route is best for you.

FORMAT YOUR BOOK YOURSELF

A book formatter charges between $40 and $250, depending on the length of your book and your requirements. For example, if your book has a lot of images or if you want special design features, it will typically cost more. By formatting your book yourself, you save on this expense.

A second advantage of formatting your own book is control. This is important when you want to make changes to your book. You may not want to go back to your formatter each time you need to upload a new version to Amazon.

However, there are downsides to doing it yourself. It takes time to format a book. There is a learning curve and if you are a perfectionist, you may find the experience frustrating. Also, if you are not detail oriented, I suggest you leave formatting to the professionals.

In summary, if you have the time and want to retain control of your formatting, then do it yourself. If this is not the case, then hire someone to format your book for you.

Here are the high level steps to format your book using Microsoft Word. This approach uses a KDP tool called *Kindle Create Add-in for Microsoft Word*. I like this tool because it's easy to learn and can be used to create a file for both eBook and paperback. The following instructions assume you are familiar with Microsoft Word.

1. Start by downloading the *Kindle Create Add-In* tool from [Amazon's help pages](). This adds a new Kindle tab to Microsoft Word.
2. Open your manuscript in Word and click the Kindle tab.
3. Click *Get Started*. This will set up trim size, margins, font size, and indentations. You can also select a theme for your book.
4. Click *Insert Template Page* to add a title page, copyright page, and table of contents.
5. Format chapter titles by placing your cursor next to each chapter title and clicking *Chapter Title*.

6. You can also format other book elements. For example, *Chapter First Paragraph* applies a drop cap to the first letter of the first word in the chapter.

7. Add page numbers by clicking *Prep for Publish* and select *Insert Page Numbers*.

8. When you're satisfied with your book, save your .doc(x) file. This is the file you will upload into KDP.

Here are some additional formatting tips:

> Make sure you remove any additional blank lines. You do not want blank lines between your paragraphs—these display as excess white space in the Kindle viewer.

> Do not include your book cover image in your manuscript file. Your cover image is uploaded to KDP separately and is automatically added when you publish your Kindle book.

> You can check the layout and formatting on a simulated device by launching *Kindle Previewer*.

The above process works if you have a text only book with no special formatting such as images, bullets, or numbered lists. If you want to go deeper, I recommend Amazon's *Kindle Create Add-In* user guide.

PAYING SOMEONE TO FORMAT YOUR BOOK

If you decide to pay a formatter, you have various options depending on your budget and requirements. As with finding an editor, you can reach out to other authors and ask for a recommendation. You can also find a freelancer on Fiverr or Upwork. We discussed both services earlier in this chapter.

Regardless of where you find your formatter, verify that your book will be formatted by hand. You do not want to pay someone to put your book through an online file conversion tool. Anyone can use these tools, and they will not fix formatting errors that are embedded in your manuscript.

Clearly communicate any special requirements up front. For example, if you want a special design for your chapter headings, you need to let the formatter know. Finally, agree on the deliverables and timeframe. At the minimum, you want your book formatted by hand and prepared for upload to Kindle. You may also want your book formatted for CreateSpace. This is a print-on-demand service. We discuss creating a physical book in chapter 15.

ACTION STEPS

1. Request some sample edits from editors you would like to work with.
2. Decide whether you want to format your book yourself or pay someone to do it for you. If you are paying someone to format your book, reach out to formatters and request a quote.

In my free [Zero To Bestseller workbook](), I share a list of professionals that I use and recommend. This includes cover designers, editors, and formatters.

Congratulations. You now have everything you need to prepare your manuscript for publishing. Next, we discuss how to write a killer book description.

CHAPTER 8

Write A Killer Book Description

What happens when someone finds your book on Amazon?

If you have nailed the cover and title, your ideal readers want to find out more. They click on your book, read your description, and check your reviews.

We cover reviews in chapter 10. For now, we will focus on crafting a book description that guarantees your ideal readers buy your book.

Your book description should tell your ideal readers what your book does for them so they will want to buy it.

BOOK DESCRIPTION FORMULA

Below is my four-step formula for creating a description that sells your book.

1. Start by defining the problem your book overcomes or the dream it fulfills. This tells your ideal readers that you understand their problems, and helps you form an immediate connection.

2. Next, paint a picture of the end result people enjoy after reading your book. Refer back to the WOW Statement you created in chapter two. What is the outcome or promise that your book delivers?

3. Give proof that your book can provide the promised outcome. For example, share specific results from your own experience or case studies from past clients.

4. Finish by including a call-to-action. Say something like "Scroll to the top and click BUY NOW to get your copy today."

Here's an example description from my first book *Make Money On Airbnb*.

1. Define the problem your book overcomes or the dream it fulfills.

> Are you looking to earn a side income without trading your time for money? Do you need a little extra to pay for family vacations, your kids' college, or next month's mortgage? Are you a stay at home mom who wants to work from home and contribute to the family finances?

2. Paint a picture of the end result your readers enjoy after reading your book.

> In this book, I'll teach you everything you need to know to list your home on Airbnb and make money fast. If you have a spare room or ever go away, you can start earning a significant side income next week.
> In this book, you'll find easy step-by-step instructions on how to:
> * Prepare your home and wow your guests.
> * Price your space and charge more than your competition.
> * Create a listing your dream guests will find irresistible.
> * Manage bookings in a few minutes each day.
> * Easily navigate the legal and financial aspects.

3. Give proof that your book can provide the promised outcome.

> In our first three months on Airbnb, our family earned on average $2,500 a month. This is without investing a single dollar and without trading our time for money.

4. Finish by including a call-to-action.

> Get your copy today by clicking the BUY NOW button at the top of this page!

By following the steps above, you will have a solid description that tells readers why they should buy your book. If you want to go further, you can add some additional selling points to your description. One that works well is scarcity.

In his book, *Influence: The Psychology of Persuasion*, Robert Cialdini describes six principles of influence. The last of these is scarcity. When people believe something is in short supply, they want it more.

As an author, you can use scarcity to motivate casual browsers to buy now instead of later. You do this by running periodic promotions, either using KDP Countdown Deals or by manually reducing your book price.

KDP Countdown Deals are available to you if you are enrolled in KDP Select. This is a program in which you agree to sell your digital book exclusively through Amazon for 90 days. In return for giving Amazon exclusivity, you earn higher royalties and can run certain promotions. There's a list of Kindle terms and their definitions in the Notes and Resources section at the end of this book.

A KDP Countdown Deal displays a countdown of the days your book will be discounted for. If you do not use a Countdown Deal, you can achieve the same result by adding a short statement to the top of your book description. For example: "Book Available at the reduced price of $0.99 for a short time only." Make sure you remember to return your book to full price at the end of your promotion. Do not use false scarcity tactics; they are unethical and ultimately turn people off.

FORMATTING YOUR BOOK DESCRIPTION

Have you noticed how some Kindle book descriptions are easier to read than others?

This is partly due to good spacing. It's advisable to keep your sentences and paragraphs short so that your book description is easy to scan. In today's busy information age, people have learned to skim text and quickly pull out the important information. You want to make sure your key selling points stand out in your book description.

You can further improve the formatting of your description by using html tags. For example, html tags allow you to create headings and emphasize words or phrases using bold or italics.

Html tags are easy to create and you do not need to be a programmer to use them. Below are some popular html tags. You can find a complete list of tags on the KDP help pages.

    <h2>This is formatted as a second level heading</h2>
    <b>This appears in bold</b>
    <em>This appears in italics</em>

This appears in italics and bold

To show you how this works, here is an example of html tags in use. The description in the KDP set-up screen reads as follows:

* Price your space and charge more than your competition.

The same description in the Amazon Kindle store looks like this:

* Price your space and **charge more than your competition**.

By using html tags, you create a well formatted book description that is easy to read.

ACTION STEPS

1. Write your book description using the four-step formula described in this chapter.
2. Include some html tags to format your description.

You are nearly ready to launch your book. In the next chapter, we will discuss pricing as well as two simple strategies to maximize your book royalties at launch and beyond.

CHAPTER 9

How To Price Your Book

*"The moment you make a mistake in pricing,
you're eating into your reputation or your profits."*
– Katharine Paine

As a self-published author, you make the decisions. This includes setting your book's price.

However, such flexibility can be overwhelming. Price too low and you miss out on higher royalties. Price too high and you attract fewer readers.

The price of your book at launch is especially important. When you first publish, you will want to maximize sales. Your goal is to build momentum in the Kindle store so that you capture the attention of the Amazon algorithms. If your book consistently attracts new readers, Amazon starts promoting it for you.

We discussed how Amazon works and the specific promotion strategies you can use in chapters three and four. In this chapter, we will focus on how to price your book at launch and beyond.

TWO LAUNCH PRICING STRATEGIES

There are multiple strategies you can follow to price your book at launch. I'm going to discuss the two approaches I believe are best. This is based on my own experience as well as discussions with multiple best-selling authors.

The first strategy uses a combination of free and 99 cent pricing. You launch your book for free, then after several days you increase the price to 99 cents. You keep the price at 99 cents for the rest of your launch period.

The free strategy helps you maximize downloads. It's much easier to convince someone to read your book for free, especially if they have not heard your name before.

The free strategy also generates more book reviews. When a person receives something for free, they are often inclined to give you something in return. One way they can do this is by reviewing your book on Amazon. Book reviews are critical to a successful launch. How to ethically request book reviews is discussed in chapter ten.

However, there are downsides to offering your book for free. The most significant shortcoming is that you attract bargain hunters. These are the people who grab your book just because it's free. Bargain hunters are more likely to leave a negative review, for example because they find your topic irrelevant or uninteresting.

I suggest you use the free strategy if you have a small or non-existent audience. By making your book free, it attracts a large number of downloads from people outside your personal network. It's also the fastest way to get reviews.

Another reason to use the free strategy is to expand your influence. My books are a source of side income, but they are also a way for me to serve people. By offering my books for free at launch, I reach a wider audience, allowing me to help more of my ideal readers.

The second approach is to launch your book at 99 cents. This launch strategy was popularized by Steve Scott in his book *Is $.99 the New Free?*

The benefit of the 99 cents approach is you deter the bargain hunters. By asking for even a small amount of money you appeal to people who want to read your book. These are your ideal readers.

However, with a paid launch, you need to work harder to attract enough downloads to get noticed by the Amazon algorithms. If you have no audience to start with, or a small one, I do not recommend launching your book at 99 cents.

ONGOING PRICING

We have discussed pricing your book at launch. But what do you do after launch?

You can keep your book at 99 cents or even offer it for free. These are both viable strategies if your goal is to reach as many readers as possible.

However, by increasing your book price you can maximize both royalties and downloads. After the initial launch period, I suggest you increase your price to $2.99. Then keep the price at this level for a few weeks before increasing it again to $3.99.

Continue raising your book price in one dollar increments until you reach a ceiling. This is the point at which you are still getting sales while maximizing profits.

For some books, $2.99 may be the best price. In other cases, you can price as high as $9.99. Your sweet spot depends on many things, including your book genre, the available competition, and your book length.

You may be wondering why I suggested starting at $2.99 and not $1.99. The main reason is KDP offers 70 percent royalties for books priced between $2.99 and $9.99. Otherwise, you earn just 35 percent. This works out at approximately 70 cents in royalties on a book priced at $1.99, and $2 on a $2.99 book. The higher percentage at the $2.99 price represents a significant jump in royalties.

One last thought on ongoing pricing. After your initial launch, you will see a drop in sales. This is inevitable. As new books hit the Kindle store, your title is pushed further down the rankings. If you see a complete drop-off in sales, you can actively promote your book until it climbs back up the best seller list.

ONGOING MARKETING

As I mentioned previously, it is no longer the case that you can rely on Amazon to sell your book for you. Even if you have a successful launch. And so, the goal of your ongoing promotion is to maintain book sales. If you do nothing after launch, your sales eventually dwindle to a handful each month. However, with a relatively small amount of effort, you can keep generating revenue each week. The key is to identify which activities work best for you and the type of books you write. Then automate these actions as much as possible.

The following is a selection of suggested strategies. Do not attempt to implement all of these. There's no one marketing strategy that guarantees your success. All the following methods take time before gaining traction. And some work better for different audiences.

Pick one or two strategies and give them your full attention for several months. If you're not seeing an increase in sales, then tweak your approach or move on to the next. Know yourself and discover what works best for you.

Your first stop should be to build an author website. If you're building a business, then you need a website. This is your home base. It's where you direct people who want to find out more about you and your work.

Your website can also help you connect with new readers. Make sure you set up an email list so that you can stay in touch with people. To find new readers, you need to implement search engine optimization (SEO). An SEO strategy helps people find your author site by telling Google (and other search engines) what your website is about. However, it's worth noting that the Internet is fairly saturated, so SEO is less effective than it was ten years ago.

Another option is to leverage the power of social media to build a large audience. However, be careful about spending too much time on social media. A large social media following doesn't always translate into more book sales and a bigger income. Research the different social media platforms to see where your potential readers are hanging out, then pick a platform and dive in.

A third way to keep promoting your books is collaboration with other authors and influencers in your niche. When you connect with people in your space, you can share your books with someone else's audience. One way to do this is by guest posting. This is when you write a post that someone else publishes on their blog.

You often receive a bio at the end of your guest post and can include a link back to your blog. This way, readers who are interested can click through and find you. It also gives you an external link to your blog, which is beneficial.

Guest posting isn't the only way to leverage someone else's audience. Being interviewed on a podcast or on a YouTube channel is a quick and easy way to connect with new people.

As you make connections in your niche and with other authors, you will also discover opportunities to collaborate. There are many ways to collaborate. For example, you can do a newsletter swap. This is where two authors promote each other's book to their email subscribers. It's a popular strategy with fiction authors who write in the same genre, such as sweet romance.

You can also take part in an online summit, organize a joint webinar, or write a round-up post in which you link to other authors' content and then ask them to share your post.

The key to a successful collaboration is to build relationships with people who have an audience like yours and who share your values. Then work together in a way that benefits everyone.

Finally, you want to consider paid advertising. This marketing strategy is not recommended for beginners. You only want to pay for advertising once you know people buy your book and have a clear picture of who your ideal readers are. If you start doing paid advertising too early, you risk spending thousands of dollars targeting the wrong people and getting zero return on your investment.

Having said that, sooner or later most successful authors realize that paid advertising is an essential component if they want to scale their business. Facebook and Amazon advertising are popular forms of paid advertising for authors. Other options include BookBub advertising, Pinterest advertising, Google AdWords, and YouTube advertising.

In all cases, you must be clear on who you are targeting, what those people want, and how you are going to get a return on your ad expenditure.

BOOK PRICING SUMMARY

Here is a summary of the different pricing strategies discussed in this chapter.

> Day zero of launch: price at 99 cents or free.
> Day three or four of launch: if your book is free, increase the price to $0.99.
> Day seven or later (end of launch period): increase your price to $2.99.
> Day 14 or later: increase your price to $3.99.

Keep increasing the price until you reach the ceiling for your book. Continue monitoring sales over the next few months. If you see a drop in sales, run a one-off promotion to boost your book back up the rankings.

ACTION STEPS

1. Decide whether you want to use the free or 99 cent launch strategy.
2. Decide how you will keep marketing your book after the initial launch.

In the next chapter, we will discuss book reviews—why they are important and how to get them.

CHAPTER 10

Why Reviews Matter And How To Get Them

Think back to the last time you purchased something online. After the price and product description, what was the next thing you looked at before buying? It was probably the reviews.

According to a survey by ChannelAdvisor, 83 percent of shoppers say that reviews affect whether they purchase a product. Online reviews are important social proof. When a shopper sees multiple positive reviews, they are more likely to buy the product.

Reviews also help your book rank higher for your selected keywords. We talked about keywords in chapter four. These are the phrases a user enters into the Amazon search bar when looking for a product. Startup Brothers claim that reviews are the most important factor in Amazon's search algorithm. If your book has a lot of four and five star reviews, it's more likely to appear high in the search results for a relevant keyword.

There is one more reason why reviews matter and that is book promotion sites. In chapter three, I explained how promotion sites are the fastest way to reach new readers. Many of the better sites require a minimum number of reviews before they accept your book. These sites want to promote quality books to their followers. Reviews are one way they can judge the quality of your book.

In short, the more reviews your book attracts, the more copies you sell.

VERIFIED VS. UNVERIFIED REVIEWS

However, not all Amazon reviews are equal. Verified reviews carry more weight in terms of both social proof and Amazon's search engine.

A verified review is a review written by someone who Amazon can confirm purchased your book. You can see which reviews are verified by looking at your book page. If a review is verified, the words "Verified Purchase" appear in orange next to the review title.

HOW TO GET BOOK REVIEWS

Now that you know why reviews are important, how do you go about attracting them?

As with many things in life, people are more likely to take action when they see others have taken the same action before them. In other words, you need to kick-start things by actively seeking reviews for your book.

The best way to do this is to create a launch team.

At the launch party for his book, *Will It Fly*, I asked Pat Flynn this question: "What one thing had the biggest impact on the success of your book launch?"

Pat replied that taking his audience along for the journey was one reason for his book's success. He went on to say that if you do not have an existing audience, you can achieve the same result with a launch team. This is a small team of people who agree to help spread the word about your book and review it on Amazon.

Pat's launch team had over 500 members. His book reached the top 100 out of all paid books while still in pre-launch phase. It went on to become a Wall Street Journal best seller.

Of course, we do not all have an audience as large as Pat's. However, we can gather a group of people who will help us launch our book. When I published my first book, I had fewer than 100 people on my email list. Nevertheless, I managed to build a launch team of 53 people. By the end of launch day, my book had over 20 reviews.

AMAZON'S TERMS AND CONDITIONS

Before we discuss how to form a launch team, it's important you understand Amazon's terms and conditions.

Amazon removes book reviews that violate the community guidelines. I have heard from authors who have seen reviews of their book disappear overnight. Often they have no idea why this happened.

It is your job to be familiar with Amazon's terms and to make sure you comply with them. You can find the KDP terms and conditions and Amazon community guidelines by searching [Amazon's KDP Help pages](#).

Amazon's guidelines include some critical information about reviews. For example, Amazon prohibits reviews that are posted in exchange for compensation. You cannot give people refunds after they download your book, offer bonus content to reviewers, or enter reviewers into a contest.

There is one exception to this rule. You can give people a free copy of your book in exchange for a review. However, you must clearly state that you welcome both positive and negative feedback when requesting a review. In addition, your reviewers must disclose that they received a free copy in exchange for their honest feedback.

YOUR LAUNCH TEAM

Now it's time to start planning your launch team. Below is my step-by-step system to form a launch team.

1. Start by creating an email list or closed Facebook Group for your team. I recommend using an email service, such as MailChimp, AWeber or ConvertKit, to collect email addresses and send your emails. Some authors create a closed Facebook Group. I prefer email because effectively managing a group takes time. Your situation may be different. Pick the method(s) you think works best for you and your launch team.

2. Plan your launch team communications in advance. Many people ask their launch team to do a range of things, including beta read their book, share it on social media, provide a testimonial, download their book, and write a review. Be careful when deciding what you want to ask your team to do. The more you ask of people, the less likely they are to take the most important action of all. I like to keep things simple. In exchange for a free copy of my book, I ask my team to download and review it at launch.

3. Engage your launch team members by sharing your progress. I send between three and five emails spread over a two- or three-week period. This is sufficient to keep people engaged without bombarding them. You may elect to share more frequently and over a longer period of time. Your approach depends on your team and the relationship you have with them.

4. Not everyone follows through and leaves a review of your book. This is normal; people get busy or they forget. I suggest you recruit at least 20 launch team members. This should be sufficient to attract at least five reviews when your book launches.

ACTION STEPS

1. Start a document and brainstorm people you can ask to join your launch team. Also include any groups you participate in. These groups are a great place to post about your book launch and recruit team members.

Make sure you keep this list handy: you will need it in the next chapter. You are finally ready to hit the *publish* button. Coming up is the final process to launch your book and become a best-selling author.

CHAPTER 11

Pulling It All Together – Your Book Launch

As I double-check the information I entered, my heart beats a little faster. This is it.

I click "Save and Publish." My first thought is, "Help! How do I un-publish?"

Publishing a book can be terrifying, and negative thoughts often compete for your attention.

What if nobody buys your book? What if people hate it? What if all the time spent writing your book was for nothing?

Having a launch plan helps you push through these fears. Having *the right plan* guarantees your success. In this chapter, you learn how to apply the strategies discussed to launch your book and reach thousands of readers.

My launch plan is just four weeks from start to finish. I skip many of the steps that other self-published authors recommend. This is because I believe in the Pareto Principle: 80 percent of results stem from 20 percent of activities.

If Kindle publishing is a source of side income for you, like it is for me, then you don't have any time to waste. I'm going to help you focus on those activities that make you more money in less time.

YOUR STEP-BY-STEP LAUNCH PLAN

The following is the exact strategy I used to get my first book to the top of multiple categories. It also reached the top 2,000 of all paid books and continues to sell every day. And it hasn't just worked for me. Through writing and coaching, I've helped thousands of other authors self-publish their first book and reach bestselling status.

The following is the free and 99 cents strategy discussed in chapter nine. Unless you have a large audience, starting out free is the best way to attract reviews at launch. It also helps you reach more of your ideal readers and make a bigger impact with your book.

STEP 1: BUILD YOUR AUTHOR PLATFORM

(Approximately four weeks prior to launch)

Your author platform is your website and email list. If you want to make more money from your books, an email list is essential. In order to build an email list, you need a basic website to send people to so they can sign up.

We discuss why you need an author platform and how to build one in chapters 12 through 14. For now, we focus on the tasks you need to do before you launch your book. There are three tasks.

1. Create Email List: If you do not already have an email list, sign up with an email provider, such as MailChimp, Mailerlite, or ConvertKit.

2. Create Bonus Landing Page: This is a page on your website that you link to in your book. The idea is you offer readers a relevant bonus in exchange for joining your email list.

3. Create Book Sales Page: This is a page on your website that links to your Amazon book page. You share this page on social media and other places when you start promoting your book.

Bonus Tip: If you sign up for Amazon's Associates program, you can use an affiliate link to your Amazon book page and earn some extra money every time someone clicks on the link and makes a purchase. I will further explain affiliate sales in chapter 15.

STEP 2: CREATE BOOK COVER, EDIT AND FORMAT BOOK

(Approximately four weeks prior to launch)

In this step, you prepare your manuscript for publishing. There are four tasks.

1. Create Book Cover: Write a design brief and send it to a handful of cover designers. Refer to chapter six for more detail on how to do this.

2. Edit Book: Follow the steps in chapter seven to select a book editor. Make sure you agree to a timeline before sending the manuscript to your editor.

3. Format Book: When you have the final version of your manuscript, format your book yourself or send it to your formatter. Chapter seven discusses how to get your book formatted.

4. Review Final Book in the Kindle Previewer: Once you have a formatted book, preview it in different Kindle formats. Make sure there are no formatting issues such as random blank pages. You can do this by uploading your book to KDP and using the viewer inside KDP. Alternatively, you can download the Kindle Previewer direct to your desktop. Be sure to save your book in draft mode, because you are not ready to publish yet.

STEP 3: CREATE LAUNCH TEAM

(Approximately four weeks prior to launch)

We discussed your launch team in the previous chapter. The primary goal for your launch team is to attract some early book reviews. The tasks are:

1. Create Launch Team Messages: Launch time can get busy, so I recommend writing your launch team emails in advance. Then all you have to do is copy and paste when it's time to send them out.

2. Recruit Launch Team Members: Start recruiting people to your launch team. You can post on social media, ask in Facebook groups, or contact your email list.

STEP 4: PRE-LAUNCH MARKETING

(Approximately three weeks prior to launch)

Next, start spreading the word about your new book. The tasks are:

1. Email Your Launch Team: Engage your launch team by sharing your progress and letting people know what you expect from them. Also, send an advance reader copy of your book. The easiest way to do this is to save your book in PDF format. Email it as an attachment or share a link to a location where it can be downloaded.

2. Submit Book To Promotion Sites: Start applying for promotions about two weeks prior to your planned launch date. Some sites require at least five reviews. If this is the case, wait until you have started stealth mode (see below).

3. Post on Social Media: Start spreading the word about your upcoming launch by posting about your book on social media.

4. Contact Influencers: Reach out to influencers to let them know about your book and to seek opportunities to share your book with their audience. Chapter three discussed ways you can do this.

STEP 5: SET UP KDP

(Approximately two weeks prior to launch)

In this step, you upload your book to KDP.

1. Create KDP Account: If you are new to KDP, visit Amazon's KDP site and create an account. The process is straightforward and only takes a few minutes.

2. Select Keywords and Categories: Select the keywords and categories for your book. We discussed how to do this in chapter four.

3. Write Book Description: Make sure you have your book description ready to go. You learned how to write a book description in chapter eight.

4. Upload Book to KDP: Once you have everything ready, upload your book to KDP and click publish. Price your book at $4.99 or higher. You do not want anyone to buy your book while you are viewing it in stealth mode. In step six, you will learn more about stealth mode. Note that Amazon can take 12 to 24 hours to review your book and publish it.

STEP 6: STEALTH MODE

(One week prior to launch)

When your book is in stealth mode, it's live in Amazon's Kindle store. Casual shoppers may find and buy your book. However, this is unlikely since during your stealth period you do no active promotion. Stealth mode is nothing more than publishing prior to your actual launch date without publicizing your book.

The goal of stealth mode is two-fold. First, you check that everything is uploaded correctly to Amazon. Second, you encourage select people to download and review your book. You want a handful of early reviews to help you submit your book to promotion sites. Stealth mode ends on your launch day. This is when you are finally ready to tell the world about your new book.

1. Check Book in KDP and change price to $0.99: Check the book cover and book description. Then buy your book and view it on different devices. If everything looks good, change the price to $0.99. By setting the price low, some of your launch team will purchase and review your book during stealth mode. Remember, you are not actively promoting your book at this point. Instead, you are working to get everything set up for your official launch day.

2. Email Launch Team: Send your launch team a link to your Amazon book page. Ask them to download and review your book now or on launch day (when it's free). A small number will buy your book for 99 cents and review it straight away. Be sure to thank these people. Getting five or more reviews while you are still in stealth mode is required to get your book accepted by some of the better promotion sites. If necessary, you can personally contact a few people to encourage them to leave a review on Amazon.

3. Set up KDP Select Promotion: This is how you launch your book for free. Schedule a free KDP Select promotion (you have to enroll your book in KDP Select first). The start date of the free promotion is your launch day. KDP Select is a program in which you agree to sell your digital book exclusively through Amazon for 90 days. In return for giving Amazon exclusivity, you earn higher royalties and can run certain promotions. You can still distribute your book in physical format through other channels. When you enroll a book in KDP Select, it is automatically included in Kindle Unlimited (KU) and the Kindle Owners' Lending Library (KOLL). There's a list of Kindle terms and their definitions in the Notes And Resources section at the end of this book.

4. Raise Book Price: About 24 hours before your free promotion is scheduled to begin, change your book price to $4.99 or higher. During your free promotion,

Amazon displays the original $4.99 price with a strike-through. This shows shoppers the value of your promotion.

STEP 7: LAUNCH DAY

Launch day is an exciting time. And if you've followed this step-by-step plan, there are only a handful of tasks to complete. They are:

1. Check Book is Free on Amazon: Amazon operates on Pacific Time, so your book should automatically become free at around midnight Pacific Time on your launch day. It may not switch at exactly midnight. Some authors report that their promotions started as much as one hour late.

2. Email Launch Team: Tell your launch team that your book is now free. Remind them to download and review it if they haven't already done so.

3. Post on Social Media: Spread the word about your book via social media and in any relevant online communities. Emphasize that your book is free for a short time only.

4. Check Scheduled Promotions: Make sure that any promotions you scheduled with book promotion sites go ahead as planned.

STEP 8: POST LAUNCH DAY

Congratulations, you published your book! However, you're not done yet. You still have a few more tasks to maximize your sales and profits.

1. Message Launch Team Individually: Thank every member of your launch team.

2. End Free Promotion and Start $0.99 Promotion: On day three or four, manually change your book price to $0.99. The goal of your free book promotion is to reach more people and to get book reviews. The aim of your 99 cent promotion is to climb the best seller ranks in the paid charts.

3. Check Scheduled Promotions: Make sure the 99 cent promotions you scheduled with promotion sites go ahead as planned. Ideally, you should have two or more promotions scheduled over several days.

4. Increase Book Price to $2.99: After a week or more, increase your book price to $2.99. The exact timing depends on your scheduled book promotions and how well your book is doing in the paid charts. The optimal time to increase your price is when your book is still climbing the rankings.

TWO CASE STUDIES

You may be wondering what results you can realistically expect when you launch your nonfiction book. Below are two case studies showing the exact numbers from two separate book launches. Both were first time books from unknown authors. The two authors followed the above launch strategy.

As your following grows, you can expect to sell even more books each time you publish a new title. As at the start of 2018, over 16,000 readers have downloaded my books. Each launch has been more successful than the previous one.

Here are the results from the launch of my first book, *Make Money On Airbnb*:

>   Day One: 374 free downloads
>   Day Two: 747 free downloads
>   Day Three: 385 free downloads, 58 sales at $0.99
>   Days Four to 10: 213 sales at $0.99
>   Total In 10-Day Launch Period: 1,429 free downloads and 271 $0.99 sales.

The highest ranking in the free store was #168 and the highest ranking in the paid store was around #2,000.

Deidre's book, *Toolkit For Wellness,* launched around the Thanksgiving Holiday. Her 99 cent period was longer due to challenges lining up promotion sites over the busy holiday period.

>   Day One: 417 free downloads
>   Day Two: 364 free downloads
>   Day Three: 354 free downloads
>   Day Four: 31 free downloads, 6 sales at $0.99
>   Days Five to 20: 195 sales at $0.99
>   Total In 20-Day Launch Period: 1,166 free downloads and 201 $0.99 sales.

ACTION STEPS

1. Choose your launch date and create your launch plan following the steps in this chapter. There are many activities to do over your four-week launch period. Having a plan is the best way to keep track of them all.

This brings us to the end of step two in the four-step system. You have everything you need to find your ideal readers and successfully sell your nonfiction book. In the next two sections, you will learn how to increase your income by building a loyal following and converting readers into repeat customers.

PART THREE

Step Three: Build Your Following

CHAPTER 12

Why You Need A Following And How To Build One

This is the story of Joshie the Giraffe.

Joshie is the beloved toy of a little boy. One day, Joshie takes a trip to Florida with his family, where they stay at the Ritz-Carlton on Amelia Island.

When the family departs, they accidentally leave Joshie behind. As any parent knows, it can be devastating when a small child loses a beloved toy. The boy's father, Chris Hurn, does what any parent would do. He tells his young son that Joshie is fine and is taking an extended vacation at the hotel.

That evening, the Ritz-Carlton calls to say they have found Joshie. Chris asks the hotel if they would mind taking a picture of Joshie on a lounger by the pool. The hotel agrees to do this, backing up the story Chris has told his son.

A few days later, a package arrives. The parcel contains Joshie, along with some Ritz-Carlton goodies, including a Frisbee and a football. Also in the package is a binder that documents Joshie's extended stay at the hotel.

It includes photographs of Joshie sunbathing by the pool, having a massage at the spa, meeting with other friends, and driving to the beach in a buggy. Joshie even receives a Ritz-Carlton I.D. badge and is made an honorary member of the Loss Prevention Team.

In this example, the Ritz-Carlton Hotel goes above and beyond to help the Hurn family. As a result, Chris and his family are now loyal customers. Furthermore, the hotel gains incredible exposure as Chris shares his experience online and the story goes viral.

Inspiring loyalty reaps massive rewards. In the coming chapters, I will teach you how to build your loyal following and serve them through your books, products, and services. By following the steps outlined in these pages, you can more than triple your income. If you address a real need and help people meet this need, you can expect to earn four or five figures in your first year, and maybe even increase it to a six-figure income. Here is how one author earns six figures.

Joanna Penn writes fiction and nonfiction books. She also has a popular blog called *The Creative Penn*.

In 2014 and 2015, Joanna's six-figure income broke down as follows:

> 50 percent book related income.
> 12 percent course sales from her website.
> 25 percent affiliate sales (commission on selling other people's products).
> 10 percent paid professional speaking.
> 3 percent sponsorship from her podcast.

Notice how Joanna earns an income from multiple sources, including courses, speaking, and affiliate sales. Yet, 50 percent of her earnings come directly from her books. Of course, this kind of success does not happen immediately. It takes time to build a following and create new books, products, and services for your audience. Joanna self-published her first book in 2008.

There is one critical piece that contributes to her success. In an article that discusses her 2016 goals, Joanna stated that she plans to focus on her email list. She explained how the size of her audience directly impacts her income.

This is important. If you want to be ahead of the game, you need to start building an engaged email list now.

BUILDING AN EMAIL LIST THE RIGHT WAY

How do you attract a loyal following of readers who want to buy from you again and again?

Remember the book funnel. First, you write a quality book that fulfills a need. This is what Joanna does with her fiction and nonfiction books. Then, you focus on attracting your ideal readers and encouraging them to sign up for your email newsletter. You seek out people who love what you have to offer and build a relationship with them over time. A proportion of your subscribers become loyal followers and eventually repeat customers.

> This is not about sending people unsolicited email. It's about building a tribe. A group of people you can help and who love what you do.

When you build an email list the right way, you always have customers ready to buy your offerings. Here is how the book funnel works in practice:

1. Someone reads your book and enjoys it.

2. In your book, you have a page that tells your reader about your bonus material. You invite the reader to visit a website page to access the bonus material.

3. The reader likes the sound of your free bonus and visits the website page. On that page, they are asked to enter their email address. When they do so, they receive immediate access to the promised bonus.

4. The person has now been added to your email list. Over time, you send them helpful emails that relate to the topic of your book(s). You offer as much valuable content as you can.

5. After a number of emails, you share a new book, product, or service that you think the person may be interested in. By now, they know you and trust you, so they're more likely to buy your product.

This sounds straightforward. However, there are some challenges.

> How do you quickly grow your email list?
> Why do people open some emails and not others?
> How do you sell in an email in a genuine and respectful way?

The secret is to offer your email subscribers unbeatable value. Teach them everything you know. Do not be afraid to give away too much for free. Get this right and your subscribers become loyal customers for life.

In the next two sections, I will teach you the exact steps to do this. In chapter 13, you will discover how to create an irresistible offer that convinces readers to join your list. Then, chapter 14 will show you the mechanics of creating your email list and a website. Finally, chapters 15 through 18 will discuss how to engage your subscribers over time so that people not only open and read your emails, but also purchase your offerings.

The beauty of the book sales funnel is that it starts with a purchase. Your ideal readers commit time and money to reading your book. From here, it is a relatively small step to converting those readers into loyal followers.

Does this sound exciting? It should. If you follow the steps in the coming chapters, you will multiply your income and gain more freedom to write books, spend time with your kids, and start new projects.

CHAPTER 13

The Perfect Email Opt-In Offer

"Email is king. It's the best way to build an engaged audience, sell a product online, or create hype around your next big event or service project. Without it, you will really struggle to get the kind of traction your message deserves." – Jeff Goins

The above is a quote from Jeff Goins, author of five books including the best sellers, *The Art of Work* and *Real Artists Don't Starve*.

So how do you convert readers into email subscribers? People are protective about their in-boxes, which means a simple request to sign up for an email list is not going to generate results. People need an incentive to invite you in.

Your opt-in offer is that incentive. Here is a definition of an opt-in offer (also known as a lead magnet):

> An opt-in offer is an offer in exchange for the right to email someone.

One online business owner told me her email opt-in rate increased fivefold when she added a lead magnet. There is no doubt that opt-in offers work. However, there is a right way and a wrong way to do it.

The wrong way may increase your number of subscribers. But this is pointless unless your subscribers are your ideal readers and unless you follow through with them.

Think about this. What happens when you meet someone at a party?

They are charming and you cannot help liking them. You schedule time to meet them again and this time they ignore you because they're too busy talking to another person. You feel disappointed and maybe even angry when you discover they didn't follow through.

Do not make this mistake with your email list. If you do, people stop opening your emails and eventually unsubscribe. We'll talk more about follow-through and how to provide ongoing value in the upcoming chapters.

Another important role of your opt-in offer is to attract more of the *right subscribers*. You do not want just anyone on your email list. You want your ideal readers, the people you can help and who love what you have to offer.

Lastly, your opt-in offer is the first step in building trust. Think back to the party example and consider how easy it is to form an opinion about someone at the initial meeting. Your opt-in offer is your chance to form a good first impression.

In summary, the right opt-in offer (coupled with ongoing value) attracts more of the right subscribers which in turn helps you sell more books and other offerings.

In this chapter, you'll learn how to create an opt-in offer that is irresistible to your ideal readers.

FEATURES OF THE PERFECT OPT-IN OFFER

The perfect email opt-in offer has four features:
1. It is desirable to your ideal readers.
Think back to your WOW Statement. What outcome do your readers want? How can you help them achieve this outcome?

Some ideas are:
> A free audio version of your book.
> A printable workbook that complements the exercises in your book.
> A free training series.
> Excel spreadsheets.
> Copy and paste templates.
> Audio interviews with experts in your field.

Make sure the offer is something you cannot easily include in your book. It needs to be something that complements your book but goes beyond the printed word. Readers feel cheated if you ask them to subscribe to your email list for something that could have been incorporated into your book.

This is why video, audio, and spreadsheets make good bonus resources. They are all formats that cannot be easily included in a Kindle book.

2. The perfect opt-in offer provides a quick win.

Your offer should deliver fast results and be easy to consume. I do not recommend offering a 100-page e-book as a bonus. I have dozens of e-books on my virtual shelf that I have not found time to read. You want your subscribers to use your opt-in offer and benefit from it.

For example, the [Zero To Bestseller workbook](#) includes a curated list of recommended book professionals and promotion sites. This resource saves new authors hours of research time and can be used immediately.

Your offer must also be easy to implement. In other words, give your readers a quick win. Here are some examples: a how-to video, a checklist, a cheat sheet, a worksheet, a short training series.

3. The perfect opt-in offer has an enticing title.

Your offer title is important because it needs to grab the attention of your readers. Here is a strategy you can use to come up with an enticing title.

Make sure your title clearly answers these three questions:

> Who is it for?
> What problem does it solve?
> How does it solve the problem?

Below is an example to show you what I mean.

"54 Headline Hacks: A Cheat Sheet for Writing Blog Posts That Go Viral" (Boost Blog Traffic)

> Who is it for? Bloggers.
> What problem does it solve? How to write viral blog posts.
> How does it solve the problem? By giving you headline hacks you can literally copy and paste.

4. The perfect opt-in offer provides ongoing value.

Lastly, your opt-in offer must give ongoing value. Do not be that person at the party who ignores someone at the second meeting. You want to build trust over time because your goal is to convert your subscribers into repeat customers. People buy from those they know, like, and trust.

You also want to offer exclusivity to your email list. Nurture the relationship by making your subscribers feel special. You can do this by sending weekly tips or creating an online community such as a Facebook Group. Another way to provide ongoing value is through a free training series or 30-day challenge.

Now it's time to create your perfect opt-in offer.

ACTION STEPS

1. Brainstorm problems your ideal reader has that you can solve.

You already did this in chapter two. Review the outcome in your WOW Statement exercise. What is the first step toward achieving that outcome? This is your perfect opt-in offer.

2. Decide on the format for your offer. Consider what formats you can produce quickly and are easy for your ideal reader to use. Examples include a downloadable resource, an email training series, or a how-to video.

3. Next, decide on a title for your opt-in offer. Make sure your title answers these three questions:

> Who is it for?
> What problem does it solve (what desirable outcome does it deliver)?
> How does it solve the problem?

4. Finally, decide how you are going to create ongoing value for your subscribers after they join your list. Do not be tempted to skip this step. This is how you build a relationship with your subscribers and stand out from the crowd.

5. Congratulations. You are ready to go ahead and create your first opt-in offer.

The next chapter takes you step-by-step through the technical process of delivering your offer and building your email list.

CHAPTER 14

Create Your Author Website

We live in a noisy world. Each day, we're bombarded by messages—phone messages, emails, television ads, billboards. Wherever we look, there's someone announcing a product or service.

How do you break through the noise? How do you tell people about your book, product, or service?

It starts with your WOW Statement. In chapter two, you figured out who you help, what outcome you give them, and why you are different. Now you need a place to share your message and a means to stay in touch with people who respond to it. You need an author platform. At its core, your author platform is how you reach a book-buying audience.

Your platform is comprised of many things. It includes your social media accounts, like Facebook, Twitter, and GoodReads. Your contacts list, including editors, other authors, and influencers. It may incorporate offline relationships with local bookstores and reading clubs. Most importantly, it includes your website and your email list.

You may be wondering whether a self-published author needs an author website. The answer is that you don't. It is possible to publish your book and reach best-seller status without an existing audience or platform. The majority of authors I interviewed for this book had no followers when they published their first book.

However, you are not going to earn a significant income from one Kindle book. In previous chapters, we established that an engaged email list is your key to earning more money. Before you can build a loyal following, you need an author website. Your website is where your readers go to find out more about you and to join your email list.

Don't delay in building your following. As Seth Godin once said:

> *"Start today to build the platform that you will be able to use three years from now."*

YOUR AUTHOR WEBSITE

At a minimum, your author website needs to have four things:

1. Home page: This is where someone first lands if they visit your website URL.

2. Book page: A description of your book with links to your Amazon book page for people to buy your book.

3. About page: Let people get to know you and how you can help them.

4. Bonus landing page: This is the page you link to in your book. It has a description of the bonus materials you promised and a form where people enter their email address so that you can send them their freebie.

Your website can have other components, but I consider these optional. For example, you may decide to create a blog. Publishing articles on your blog demonstrates your authority in a topic and helps people discover you online. People are more likely to find your website via a Google search if you've written multiple posts on a specific topic.

However, it can be difficult to attract the attention of Google's algorithms because there are many other websites competing for top place in Google searches. Also, there are other methods to demonstrate your authority. Publishing a best-selling book is an excellent way to establish your expertise.

Lastly, a blog is time-consuming to maintain. If you have limited hours to write, I recommend you first focus on creating quality books for your book-buying audience. Then, if you have time, consider adding a blog.

HOW TO SET UP YOUR AUTHOR WEBSITE

An in-depth tutorial on building a website is beyond the scope of this book. If you need more technical help, you can reference one of the many online resources or hire a professional to create a site for you.

Having said that, it is important that you understand how a website works. As your author career develops, you want to make sure your site can grow with you.

Below are the high level steps to creating a website:

1. Select a website host. Your host is the company that provides an area on the Internet where the files that make up your website live. Hosting services start at around $3 per month. For new authors, I recommend FastComet. You can visit their website and sign up for a hosting account in less than a minute.

2. Install WordPress. I recommend you use Wordpress.org to build your site. It is the most established website building platform and it's easy to find online help if you get stuck creating your site. There are also many professional website developers who are well-versed in WordPress. Most hosting services have a one-click WordPress install.

3. Select a theme. This is the look and feel of your website. I use the Genesis Framework. It is flexible and has great looking themes. However, it comes at a price. You may prefer to start with one of the many free alternatives that provide attractive and responsive themes. You can browse free themes by visiting "Themes" under the "Appearance" menu in your WordPress dashboard. Make sure you select a responsive theme. This is a theme that adapts to mobile and other platforms.

4. Create your website pages. Log on to your WordPress site and create the pages you need. For example: Home Page, About Page, Book Bonus Page, and Book Page. Also create a menu so that people can navigate to these pages within your site.

5. Sign up for an email service provider. Create an email list and add sign-up forms to your site. An email service provider allows you to send bulk emails. When starting out, I recommend you use a service like MailChimp, AWeber, or ConvertKit. All of these services provide online help that shows you how to create a list and add sign-up forms to your website.

You now have a basic author website. However, you are not done yet. Next, optimize your site so that you can build your email list more quickly and start making more money.

EASY WEBSITE TWEAKS TO QUICKLY INCREASE EMAIL OPT-INS

Everything about your website must appeal to your ideal reader. Invite them to stick around, subscribe to your email list, and buy your books, services, or products.

The main goal of your website is to convert website visitors into email subscribers. There are five main places you can ask for an opt-in.

1. Your Home Page

This is often the first place your website visitors see. Your homepage must tell the visitor what you offer in five seconds or less. Refer back to the WOW Statement you created in chapter two. Make sure your website tells visitors who you help, the outcome or promise they can expect, and why you are unique.

Your home page should also have a prominent email opt-in form or button above the fold. This means it should be visible without having to scroll down the page.

2. Your About Page

Your about page is typically one of your most visited pages, making it the perfect opportunity to ask for the opt-in. Make sure your about page includes a descriptive headline, something more than "About Us" or "About."

Tell your ideal reader what you offer them. Make it about them before you talk about yourself. This is the most common mistake I see on about pages. The website owner talks about themself but never mentions what they offer their audience.

Lastly, include at least one email opt-in form or button on your about page. Once people become excited about who you are, and how you can help them, give them a chance to stay in touch by joining your email list.

3. Your Blog Posts

If your website has a blog, add an email opt-in form to the end of your blog posts. If a visitor reads a post all the way to the end, then she likes your content. Make sure you take advantage of this by asking for the email opt-in.

4. Pop-Up Box (optional)

Pop-ups increase opt-ins. Nevertheless, I understand that some people find these annoying and it is your choice whether you want to use one.

If you do decide to include a pop-up box on your site, make sure you succinctly describe the benefit or outcome your subscriber can expect. Minimize annoyance, for example, by setting a timer and frequency. You might configure your pop-up to only appear to the same user once every 14 days.

5. Bonus Landing Page

This is the page where someone signs up to receive the free bonus you offer in your book. You can view the bonus page for this book at sallyannmiller.com/ztb.

ACTION STEPS

1. If you do not already have a site, follow the steps in this chapter to set up your author website.

2. Once you have a website, apply the easy website tweaks above to increase your email opt-ins.

This brings us to the end of step three in the four-step system. Now, you know how to build your following by creating an email list. In the final section, we will discuss how to convert your subscribers into loyal followers who are eager to buy your books, products, and services.

PART FOUR

Step Four: Make More Money

CHAPTER 15

10 Ways To Make More Money

We have explored how to find your ideal readers and encourage them to buy your book. You also know how to invite those readers to join your email newsletter.

The next question is, what do you do with your email list?

This chapter will discuss new offerings you can present to your subscribers. Think of this as a menu of options. You get to pick one or two offerings you can create for your tribe.

At this point, you may be crying out, *"I'm an author. I want to make money selling books!"*

Selling more books is one approach. However, it's not your only option and it's not always the most lucrative. In this chapter, I will present ten ways to make more money from your nonfiction books.

If you're reluctant to try something new, think about this. Your audience wants to hear from you. They have needs and dreams that you can fulfill. By offering new books, products, or services, you are helping the people you most want to serve.

Remember that nothing is permanent. If you try something and it doesn't work, you can always move on to the next idea. You never know when a new and exciting opportunity may open up to you.

1. AFFILIATE SALES OF YOUR BOOK

There are a few quick and easy ways you can maximize your earnings from your published book. One such way is to sign up for an Amazon Associates account and earn affiliate income on the sales of your book.

Once you get an Amazon Associates account, you will obtain a special link to your Amazon book page. You place this link on your website. Every time someone clicks through and buys your book, you earn a small commission.

The commission on a book sale is just a few cents, but if that same person goes on to buy other products on Amazon, then you also receive a commission on *those* sales. If you are lucky and they buy a TV or computer, that's a nice bit of extra cash. For example, someone once purchased a dehumidifier valued at $220 after clicking on my affiliate link. I earned $8.80 on this sale. Every little bit helps!

Make sure you are familiar with Amazon's terms and conditions. For example, Amazon does not allow you to include Amazon Associate links in your ebooks. Nor can you purchase on your own behalf through your affiliate link.

You can, however, include affiliate links to non-Amazon products in your ebooks. We discuss this further in option six below.

2. PHYSICAL BOOK

The next easiest thing you can do is create a physical version of your book. Amazon makes this relatively straightforward through the KDP platform.

KDP is a print-on-demand service. You do not need to pay upfront to have books printed and stored in a warehouse. You upload your book to their platform and after a review process it's automatically displayed on your Amazon book page.

I use KDP to self-publish my paperback books. It's easy to learn and I like having all my book sales reported in one place (in KDP Reports). Amazon has extensive help pages that walk you through how to create and upload your paperback book.

As well as giving you one more revenue stream, there is a second advantage. Your Amazon page displays both the paperback and the kindle versions of your book. Since your paperback book is higher priced, your Kindle version appears more valuable.

3. AUDIOBOOK

Audiobooks are a rapidly growing industry that cannot be ignored. According to the Audio Publisher's Association, in 2016 audiobook unit sales increased by almost 20 percent. Their research also revealed that "24 percent of Americans (more than 67 million people) have completed at least one audiobook in the last year."

You can sell your audiobook via Amazon's Audible platform. You have three options to record your book. You can make a recording at home, hire a sound studio, or utilize Amazon's Audiobook Creation Exchange (ACX).

ACX matches you up with a professional voice reader. You either pay them upon completion of the audiobook or split all royalties with them fifty-fifty. An audiobook you make on ACX is available on Audible.com, Amazon.com, and iTunes. If you grant Audible exclusive distribution rights, you earn royalties of 40 percent.

Having your book on Audible exposes you to a wider reader base as well as giving you a new source of income. Furthermore, you can make an extra $50 through the ACX bounty program every time your audiobook is the first purchase of a new Audible listener.

I released my first audiobook in December 2017. I sold 71 copies in the first two months. This was without any active promotion. I simply hired an actor to record my book, reviewed their recording, and published.

4. MORE BOOK TITLES

Each new title you publish provides an extra income stream and boosts sales of your previous books. As new readers discover you, some want to buy your other titles. This strategy is effective if you have multiple books in the same genre. It can also work if you branch out into new topics. Sometimes a reader enjoys your style and wants to buy everything you write.

If you have multiple titles, make sure you have an Amazon Author Central page that links them together. This is a free page on the Amazon website. Once you have a published title, you can build your Author Page by signing up on Amazon Author Central. Fill in the page with information including a biography, booklist, and more. Another way to help readers find your books is to put links to your other titles at the end of each book.

5. BOOK BUNDLE

Once you have multiple book titles, you can create a book bundle. This is a group of related titles that are sold as a set. It involves compiling several books you've already published into a single book set. A new formatted file and a new book cover will have to be created for your bundle. Then, publish your bundle as you would any other book.

Another option is to create a book bundle with other authors. In this case, you partner with one or more authors to market your bundle. This is an excellent way to reach a new audience who may not otherwise discover your books.

6. OTHER PEOPLE'S PRODUCTS

We have already discussed how you can earn commission through Amazon's Associates program. You can also make money as an affiliate for other people's products.

When you sign up for an affiliate program, you receive an affiliate link. You can place this link on your website, in your emails, or in your e-books (though make sure you familiarize yourself with the program's terms and conditions). Every time someone clicks on the link and makes a purchase, you earn a commission on the sale. There is no additional cost to the customer.

If you are new to affiliate sales, you may be surprised to discover how many options exist. For example, did you know Target has an affiliate program?

To find affiliate programs, simply Google the name of a business you are interested in and the phrase "affiliate program." You can also check the footer or menu options on different business websites.

Make sure you only promote products you personally use that are relevant to your audience. Remember, you are building a relationship with your email subscribers. The last thing you want to do is spam them with low quality products.

7. DIGITAL TRAINING PRODUCT

Perhaps you are not comfortable promoting someone else's products. Or maybe you feel you can create something better that your audience will love. If this is the case, go for it! Options seven through 10 are all about selling your own products and services.

As a nonfiction author, one obvious choice is to create a training program that goes deeper into your book topic. There are many ways to create and sell a training program. You can leverage an existing platform that already has thousands of course buyers. Udemy is one such platform.

Alternatively, you can deliver your course via your own website. Some ways to do this are:

> An email course. For this, you'll need an email service that has auto-responder or drip feed functionality. Chapter 18 will discuss how to create an email series.

> An ebook sold from your website using a PayPal button or via a service like Gumroad.

> A course built on an all-in-one platform such as Teachable or Podia.

> A self-hosted video course. This is a little more complex to set up. It requires you to create a membership site and pay for a video hosting service. I have done this before using a WordPress plugin called WishList Member. This is a plugin that turns your website into a membership site where users log in to access course content. For video hosting, I used a company called Vimeo.

8. IN-PERSON TRAINING PRODUCT

You may prefer to connect in-person with your audience. In this case, you can create an event. This could be a 10-person seminar at your local church or a thousand-person conference at a large hotel. Other ideas include a retreat or workshop.

Deidre, author of *Toolkit For Wellness*, started out holding Designed for Health Seminars. These were free seminars hosted at her local church. Now that Deidre has published a book and has a growing following, she plans to create a paid version of the seminar.

9. ONE-ON-ONE SERVICE

Another option is to offer a one-on-one service. These can be high value and are ideal if you are called to help people at a personal level.

Many nonfiction authors offer a coaching service that relates to their topic. If you are new to coaching, I recommend you start by offering your services for free or at a discount. This allows you to gain experience, test out your idea, and gather some early testimonials. As you become recognized in your niche, you can charge anywhere from $50 to over $1,000 per coaching session.

If coaching is not your thing, you can offer a different type of service. For example, I used to offer a website review service. I helped people convert website visitors into email subscribers and customers. I presented my clients with a 15-minute video and a written report of my recommendations.

10. SPEAKING

Lastly, you can seek opportunities to get paid as a speaker. As with coaching, you may start out at a low speaking rate or for free. As you build your reputation, you can increase your rates.

For many, speaking is immensely rewarding. It is also an effective way to reach a new book-buying audience. This is what Marcy Pusey did when she visited California for a friend's wedding. Marcy was invited to speak at an Orphan Care Summit as the close-out speaker. She brought along copies of her recently published book, *Reclaiming Hope*. At the event, Marcy sold every physical copy she had with her and more. During her trip, she earned $600 in physical book sales.

Marcy told me, "Having a published book opens doors. It gives you a professional voice and credibility."

ACTION STEPS

1. Read through the above ideas. Also research the products and services other authors in your field offer.

2. Decide on one or two offerings you want to create for your ideal readers.

I hope this chapter has you inspired to serve your audience more deeply. In the next three chapters, you will learn exactly how to introduce your offerings to your audience and start earning more money.

CHAPTER 16

Why People Read Some Emails But Not Others

According to MailChimp, the average email open rate in Media and Publishing is 22.3 percent. This means that approximately four out of five email subscribers do not open email newsletters.

However, you are not average. The next three chapters will cover how to build an ongoing relationship with your subscribers.

My email open rate is around 30 percent. For a past business, it was over 50 percent. Yours may be lower or higher. Open rates vary based on your field and the number of people on your list. As a benchmark, I recommend you aim for an open rate of at least 30 percent when starting out. This number will drop as your list grows beyond the first 1000 subscribers.

Here are four ways you can improve your open rate.

1. BE CONSISTENT

Do you remember the story about the hare and the tortoise?

The hare brags about his speed to a slow-moving tortoise. So the tortoise challenges the hare to a race. Partway through the race, the hare decides to take a nap. He is confident he will win and believes he can afford to take a break. While the hare sleeps, the tortoise steadily crawls past the hare and crosses the finish line first.

In this story, consistency pays off. The same is true for your business.

Be consistent in your writing style. Pick a style that suits you and your audience, then stick with it. I recommend adopting a personal tone – be you and show that you care about your subscribers. The closer your writing is to your true voice, the more your subscribers connect with you and your message. This is especially true today. People are inundated by messages and are on high alert for sales offers.

Also, decide on a consistent theme for your emails. This is important when you are building up to a new offering. Your aim is to take your subscribers on a journey. This journey starts with your opt-in offer and continues with a series of related emails before finishing with your offering. We'll discuss how to write a sequence of emails that sell in the next two chapters.

Lastly, you want to be consistent in the timing and frequency of your emails. How often you send emails depends on you and your audience.

Some people send daily emails. This is aggressive but can be effective. For example, Brian Tracy, motivational speaker and author, sends his subscribers a daily inspirational quote. You may prefer to send weekly or monthly emails. Whatever you decide, tell your subscribers what to expect and be consistent.

2. USE "OPEN ME" SUBJECT LINES

Your subject line is the first step in getting someone to open your email. If you write a bad subject line, all but your most loyal subscribers will hit the delete button.

What works for you may be different from what works for me. The answer is to experiment and see which subject lines get the most people to open the email. You can find out how many times a specific email is opened in the reports section of your email provider.

To help you get started, you will find five subject lines below that are proven to work in most categories. For each example, there is a simple template you can use to construct your email subject lines.

1. The curiosity subject line. This works by presenting a question that begs for an answer. For example: "The surprising truth about [topic]."

2. A solution to an urgent problem. If your subscribers are experiencing this problem, they want to read your answer. For example: "How to achieve [benefit] without [something tedious]."

3. How to avoid a fear. Similar to number two, your subscribers want to hear your solution. For example: "Five reasons why [fear] and what you can do about it."

4. The controversial subject line. This one uses surprise to grab the reader's attention. For example: "Why [common belief] is not true."

5. Lists and numbers. Lists are eye catching and promise a quick and easy read. For example: "Ten ways to do [something your audience cares about]."

3. ENGAGE YOUR IDEAL READERS

The third way to get your emails opened is to consistently engage your subscribers. If people don't enjoy your emails, they will stop opening them. Once you attract your ideal readers, discuss the things they care about. This is how casual subscribers become loyal followers.

Loyal followers are the people who look forward to your emails. They cannot wait to read what you have to say. Many also go on to buy your books, products, and services. We explore exactly how to create engaging content in the next chapter.

4. USE OPEN LOOPS

This last strategy is surprisingly simple.

An open loop creates anticipation. It's a tactic used in television shows, movies, and books. When you are watching a television show and see a snippet of what's coming next, this is an open loop designed to keep you watching through the commercial break.

Here's an example of how it looks in an email. You close your email by saying:

> *In my next email, I'll show you how one of my clients doubled his book sales in a single month.*

If your subscribers are authors who are keen to sell more books, they will want to open your next email.

We have covered how to use consistency, subject lines, engaging content, and open loops to get your emails opened. In the next two chapters, you will learn what to write about and how to present your offerings via email.

CHAPTER 17

How To Sell More Books, Products, And Services

Picture yourself walking into a new store where you are confronted by an array of options. There are no signs and nobody around to assist you. Rather than wander aimlessly, you decide to stop wasting your time and leave.

Now imagine visiting a different establishment. This store has a wide, open entrance with signs indicating the merchandise. Someone smiles and greets you as you walk in.

Both stores offer the same products at the same price. However, one is unwelcoming and fails to engage you, while the other invites you in and leads you to the products you're looking for.

You need to be like the second store, taking your followers by the hand and leading them to your sales offerings. Let's examine how to do this via email.

BUILD KNOW, LIKE, AND TRUST FACTORS

People buy from people they like. It takes time, but you can build know, like, and trust factors with your email subscribers.

One way to do this is by using the exact language of your readers. In chapter two, I suggested writing down the words your ideal readers use. Incorporate these phrases into your emails. This helps you connect with your audience by demonstrating that you understand them.

Second, tell stories to engage people and let them get to know you. The best stories are personal. Share a little about your life and your own struggles or successes. You can also use stories from books, movies, or previous clients. If you share client stories, make sure you ask permission first. Stories engage because humans want to hear the ending. We stick around for the punch line.

Lastly, share testimonials, case studies, and customer emails (again, make sure you request permission first). All of these demonstrate that your methods work. They build trust and help your subscribers learn more about you as a person.

Here is one last tip. Imagine you are writing to a friend. When I write emails, I have a specific person in mind. She is my ideal reader and has the exact problem I can help her with. This strategy helps me create more meaningful and valuable content.

ASK SUBSCRIBERS TO TAKE ACTION

This is one of the most common questions I hear: *How do you get subscribers to take action?* It's frustrating when people fail to click on your blog posts, visit your sales page, or leave comments.

Here is my question for you: Do you ask people to take at least one action in all or most of your emails?

If not, you should start now and begin with small actions. Ask for things that are quick and easy to do. Actions may include:

> Click to read a blog post.
> Reply to a question, for example, "What Are You Struggling With?"
> Comment on a blog post.
> Forward this email to friends.
> Take a survey.
> Visit a sales page.

When you ask people to take action on a regular basis, you get them accustomed to responding to you. You also build a deeper relationship and learn how you can help them. This is valuable information when designing offerings that your subscribers will love.

I invite my audience to share their stories and struggles with me. Every day I receive emails from my subscribers and readers. Responding to these emails has become one of my favorite pastimes. Instead of seeing it as a chore, I treasure every person who takes the time to read one of my books and contact me.

THE NEXT LOGICAL STEP

You're reading this book because you want to earn more money as a nonfiction author. Yes, you love to write and help people. But you also need to pay the bills. Eventually, you want to sell something to your followers.

In some cases, you may be able to sell in your first email. However, I recommend building a relationship over time. Send at least five engaging emails before introducing your offering as the next action. In chapter 18, you will learn exactly how to do this. For now, it is important to understand what I mean by the next logical step.

You take your subscribers on a journey. At each step in the journey, you help them solve a specific problem. As they reach the end of the journey, they should already have experienced positive results. This is critical.

> *Be generous and give plenty of free value. Once you have done this, you can offer a deeper transformation through one of your paid solutions.*

By now, your subscribers like you and they trust that you can solve their problem. Some are ready to pay for your offering. It is the next logical step for your subscriber.

We have covered the theory, and now it's time to begin. In the next chapter, you will put everything you have learned into action and build an email sequence that sells.

CHAPTER 18

Make Money While You Sleep

Let me paint a picture of your future. You wake up and enjoy a cup of coffee. Perhaps you read the paper or listen to the news before heading out for a run or going to the gym. Maybe you spend an hour playing with your kids.

Once your brain is in gear, you check your email and find several messages from your payment processor.

While you slept, you made five new sales and your total earnings are $485.

This is what happened the morning I launched my first paid product to my email list. It was a video training course, priced at $97. I was not a well-known Internet guru and I did not have a large following. I now make 10 times that amount just from my book royalties.

If I can do this, you can too. In this chapter, you will learn how to make money while you sleep. Let's take a look at how it works for a nonfiction author.

Someone reads your book and subscribes to your email list. You engage them through a series of emails that leads to a paid offering. Your offering might be another book, a training course, or a one-on-one service. You present your offering over several emails linked to a sales page. Your subscriber clicks on your link and buys your new offering.

In the process described above, you take your ideal reader through all five stages of the book sales funnel:

> Ideal Reader > Book Buyer > Email Subscriber > Loyal Follower > Repeat Customer

So far, you have learned how to take readers through the first three stages. We now examine how to create loyal followers and repeat customers. It's time to build your email sequence.

PLAN YOUR EMAIL SEQUENCE

Start by choosing an overall theme for your email sequence. What problem can you solve for your audience?

A good way to do this is to work backwards from your paid offering. For example, one of my prior offerings was an email marketing course. For my email sequence, I provided a free training series. I taught five secrets to get people to open and click on your emails.

As you plan your email sequence, think about the journey you want to take your subscribers on. The journey starts with your opt-in offer and culminates in your sales offering. Along the way, you provide value and demonstrate your credentials.

Write down one or two sentences describing the content you plan to include in each email. I recommend you create a sequence of between five and 10 emails. The last two or three emails introduce your paid offering.

Ensure that every email provides something of value to your subscribers. For example, you may describe an actionable step toward solving an urgent problem or a case study describing how someone else overcame the same issue.

YOUR WELCOME EMAIL

Once you have mapped out your email content, you are ready to write the first email in your sequence. This is the welcome email. It is sent immediately after a new subscriber joins your list.

Your welcome email is special. It should do all of the following:

1. Welcome the person and thank them for joining your list.
2. Explain who you help, what outcome they can expect, and why you are different. Refer to your WOW Statement in chapter two. Make this section personal. You want to connect with your ideal readers.
3. Deliver your opt-in offer.
4. Explain what people can expect next.
5. Include a call-to-action.

Below is a sample welcome email. This is the email I send to people who opt in for one of the freebies on my website.

> Hi,
> Thank you so much for signing up. I'm excited you're here. And if you're a return customer for freebies, welcome back!
> First of all, here's the link to download your workbook:
> CLICK HERE TO GET YOUR WORKBOOK
> Now, here's a little about me...
> I'm a coach and author. I'm passionate about staying home with my kids AND earning an income. I've published five books and reached over 16,000 amazing readers... many of my readers have also become email subscribers and clients. I've also started three businesses. And have found my purpose (and a way to get paid to stay home) as an author and coach.
> Now, I want to share what I've learned (and am still learning) with you. From this point forward, I'll email you biweekly updates on my journey. I'll also send you occasional offers and freebies.
> I love helping quiet achievers make a real difference in the world. I know you have gifts to share and want to help you do amazing things.
> You can expect stories, step-by-step guides (I spent 19 years as a business analyst - so systems are kinda my thing) and a heavy dose of inspiration. I may even talk about my family and kids. Because at the end of the day, that's what matters most in my life.
> <Photo of me and my family goes here>
> And if this isn't you - that's okay. I won't be offended if you have to unsubscribe.
> But if you're still with me, fantastic!
> One last thing, would you email me back and tell me what's your biggest stumbling block with working from home?
> I read every email I receive and do my best to reply within 48 hours. So if you want some ideas to help you achieve your dreams, get in touch today!
> Wishing you all the best,
> Sally

Notice how this example hits the five points listed above. It starts out by welcoming the new subscriber. I then outline who I help and how. I include some personal information, including a picture of my family. I explain how often the new subscriber can expect to hear from me. I provide a link to my opt-in offer. Finally, I ask the person to take action by emailing me back.

WRITE YOUR FOLLOW-UP EMAILS

Now write the remainder of your emails. Remember, you want to deliver value and build up to an irresistible sales offer. To help you write your emails, I have a checklist. If you follow this formula you will write the perfect email every time.

1. Give your email an "open me" incentive in the subject line. We discussed how to do this in chapter 16.

2. Start your email by talking about an urgent problem or deep desire your readers are likely to be experiencing.

3. Include a know, like, or trust factor. For example, a case study, a personal story, or a testimonial.

4. Talk about the solution to the problem or desire you introduced at the start of the email.

5. Position your call-to-action as the next logical step. For example, link to a blog post on your website that provides a deeper discussion on the topic.

6. Check the language you use in your email. Try reading it out loud to make sure the sentences flow and your tone is consistent. Be real and be yourself

7. Check your formatting. Make sure your email is easy to scan and not a wall of text. This means short sentences and short paragraphs. I recommend no more than two or three sentences per paragraph.

8. As we discussed in the previous chapter, introduce your offering at the end of your sequence.

TEST AND REFINE

Writing great content takes time. Expect to come back and refine your emails later, but don't delay too long. You can always test what you have and tweak your emails as needed.

Once the email sequence is live, I recommend monitoring your results. Check your open rates and clicks. An open rate is the percentage of people who open your email. Clicks are the number of people who click on a link in your email. You can find this data in the reports section of your email provider. The most popular email providers, such as MailChimp, AWeber, and ConvertKit, all offer this functionality.

If an email has a low open rate, try changing your subject line. As a benchmark, I recommend aiming for an average open rate of at least 30 percent when you're starting out. This may fall as your list grows to thousands of subscribers.

If an email has too few clicks, review your content and your call-to-action. Is there a compelling reason for the person to click on the link? Have you presented it as the next logical step?

Having said this, do not obsess over opens and clicks. Your most important metric is sales. If you are making sales at the end of your sequence, then celebrate. You're helping your readers and making more money!

ACTION STEPS

1. Plan your email sequence. Decide how many emails you are going to write and what content you will deliver in each email.
2. Write your welcome email using the formula described above.
3. Write your follow-up emails using the checklist.
4. Make your email sequence live, test it, and refine.

Congratulations, you just completed the final exercise. You now have an email sequence you can send to new subscribers.

One final note: Do not send people a series of emails and then stop contacting them. Regardless of whether people buy or not, continue to send great content on a consistent basis.

After a few months, you can introduce a new sales sequence. Give people the opportunity to buy from you on a periodic basis.

Remember this: If you wait for people to find your offerings on their own, you won't make many sales. Instead, a thoughtful email sequence that builds trust over time generates a steady stream of income.

CHAPTER 19

What's Next?

Now, you understand the four-step system and it's time to take action. Here's a quick re-cap of the four steps we covered in this book:

> Step 1: Reach Your Ideal Readers. Help the right people discover your book.
> Step 2: Sell Your Book. Make your book irresistible to your ideal readers.
> Step 3: Build Your Following. Build a list of email subscribers who want to hear from you and who you can help.
> Step 4: Make More Money. Give unbeatable value and build trust over time. Then earn more money by presenting new offerings.

Perhaps you're like me and want to earn an income while you stay home with your kids. You want to be more than "just a mom." You want to share your gifts with the world and change people's lives.

Or maybe you dream of escaping your nine-to-five. You want financial freedom and a more meaningful life.

Whatever your reasons, the steps I have provided show you how to publish your book and start earning an income as an author.

If you need extra support, you can sign up for my [Zero To Bestseller]() workbook. This free workbook provides the action items and tools to help you publish your best-selling book.

If all you do is follow steps one and two of the four-step system, you can launch your best seller and earn triple the average income from a nonfiction book.

If you implement steps three and four, you can increase your earnings by two, three, or even thirty times. Recall the example from chapter one. Once you build a list of 2,000 *engaged* email subscribers, you can realistically launch a $500 product and earn $10,000 at launch.

This is quite possible. It's not difficult to build an email list of 2,000 engaged subscribers. All you need to do is follow a system and stick with it. This book offers you one such system. It is designed specifically for authors like you.

The sooner you apply the steps, the sooner you'll start seeing results. In the words of Seth Godin:

> *"What you need to do is the hard work day by day building a group of people who trust you, and want to support you when it's time."*

Your ideal readers are waiting. Go publish your best-selling book, build your following, and start earning a real income as a nonfiction author.

KINDLE TERMS

Kindle Direct Publishing (KDP): Amazon's platform that allows you to self-publish your book and offer it for sale in the Kindle store.

KDP Select: A program in which you agree to sell your digital book exclusively through Amazon for 90 days. Your book is also included in Kindle Unlimited (KU) and the Kindle Owners' Lending Library (KOLL). Lastly, enrolling in KDP Select grants you access to Kindle Countdown Deals and Free Book Promotion.

Kindle Countdown Deal: A limited-time discount promotion on your book (currently Amazon.com and Amazon.co.uk only). Customers see the regular price and promotional price on your book page. A countdown clock shows how much time is left at the promotional price.

Kindle Unlimited (KU): A subscription service available to Amazon customers in certain countries. Kindle Unlimited customers can read as many books as they like and keep them as long as they want for a monthly subscription fee.

Kindle Owners' Lending Library (KOLL): Allows Amazon Prime members to borrow one book for free each month.

Author Central: Amazon helps you create an Author Page when you sign up for Author Central. Here, you can post more information including a biography and booklist. When you first create an Author Central account, you are able to link your published Kindle books to your Author Page by searching for your author name and manually claiming each book.

Categories: Customers shopping for books in the Kindle Store can browse by genre and subgenre. These are called browse categories. You may select up to two categories for your book.

Keywords: The search terms an Amazon user may enter into the Amazon search bar when looking for books on your topic. Keywords can be a word or a phrase.

ABOUT THE AUTHOR

Sally is a mom on a mission. She is passionate about answering the question, "Can modern moms have it all?" In a previous life, Sally worked for nineteen years as a project manager and business analyst in London and Silicon Valley. She has a Bachelor's Degree in Computer Science and a Master's Degree in Business Administration.

When her daughter was born, she discovered a new purpose. Sally left her corporate career to be a stay-at-home mom. She wanted to be a full-time mom to her kids. However, she missed the freedom and purpose that came from working. So Sally made a decision: she'd find a way to stay home with her kids and earn an income (without feeling torn between the two).

Sally is a self-confessed research geek and compulsive planner. She loves learning how stuff works, mastering new skills, and sharing her knowledge with others. Since leaving her nine-to-five, Sally has published 15 books (and counting). You can find out more by visiting her website at: sallyannmiller.com.

www.ingramcontent.com/pod-product-compliance
Lightning Source LLC
Chambersburg PA
CBHW020444220526
45464CB00002B/856